HEAVEN

The Home of the Redeemed

ITS LOCATION   ITS PEOPLE
ITS CHARACTER   ITS BLISS

TWELVE IMPORTANT PAPERS
BY WRITERS OF REPUTE

COMPILED BY

HY. PICKERING

Editor of "THE WITNESS," "THE
CHRISTIAN GRAPHIC," "BOYS & GIRLS."
Author of "CHIEF MEN AMONG THE
BRETHREN," "100 WORLD-WITNESSES
TO THE COMING OF THE LORD,"
"FRESH MINTED GOLD," ETC., ETC.

PICKERING & INGLIS
LONDON   GLASGOW   EDINBURGH

LONDON - - 14 PATERNOSTER ROW, E.C.4
GLASGOW - 229 BOTHWELL STREET, C.2
EDINBURGH - 29 GEORGE IV BRIDGE, 1
NEW YORK - LOIZEAUX BROTHERS,
19 WEST 21ST STREET

Where is Heaven?

WHERE is Heaven? Is it not
        Just a friendly garden plot,
Walled with stone and roofed with sun,
Where the days pass one by one,
Not too fast and not too slow,
Looking backward as they go
At the beauties left behind
To transport the pensive mind?

Does not Heaven begin that day
When the eager heart can say:
"Surely God is in this place,
I have seen Him face to face
In the loveliness of flowers,
In the service of the showers,
And His voice has talked to me
In the sunlit apple tree?"

B. CARMAN.

Made and Printed in Great Britain

HEAVEN

SURPRISED to find how little interest seems to have been really taken, and how little seems known of **The Future Abode of the Ransomed**, we set to work to solicit the help of several of our best known writers to supply us with papers on

"WHAT ABOUT HEAVEN?"

or, "What I gather from the Word of God as to its **location, its peoples, its character, its bliss,** and other details."

THE IMPORTANCE OF "HEAVEN" in the Scriptures, can be seen by a glance at a Concordance, which shows that it is named in the Bible more than 550 times. Did not the Saviour Himself use **"Heaven"** as an incentive to prayer (Matt. 6. 9); an antidote of fear (Luke 12. 32); a stimulus to service (Matt. 5. 12); a place of rewards (Matt. 5. 12); joy for the living (Luke 6. 25); comfort for the dying (Acts 7. 56); and the hope for all (1 Thess. 1. 10).

A CONFIRMATION of the need of such papers is given by FRANKLIN FERGUSON, for many years editor of the *New Zealand Treasury*. He says: "I have been saved over 51 years, and heard much ministry yet *I have no clear recollection of hearing an address solely on Heaven*; likewise articles on the same subject are nearly as scarce. How is that? Of course, we have ministry on the Lord's Coming, and even the Judgment seat of

Christ; *why not Heaven?*   If our brethren who minister the Word would start some addresses on the place we are going to, how it might set our hearts on things above."

Another Confirmation.   A teacher whose name is known world wide replied: *"I do not know enough about Heaven to write about it."*

We sincerely trust that these articles will not only be of general interest on a subject on which ministry is needed, but that they will be of spiritual profit, and induce to more devotion of heart and service to "THE GOD OF HEAVEN" (Psa. 136. 26).

Contents

CHAPTER I

How Shall We Think of Heaven?

By GEORGE GOODMAN, Tunbridge Wells

WITH most, the idea of Heaven is very indefinite. It consists of some very blessed negatives—no more sickness, pain, or parting; and some great positives—rest, reward, and, best of all, to be with the Lord. "It's Heaven to be where Jesus is" satisfies the hunger of the soul. They are sure of this, and the rest scarcely matters by comparison. Such Scriptures as Eph. 2. 7, "That in the ages to come He might shew the exceeding riches of His grace in His kindness toward us through Jesus Christ," leaves the mind more than contented. If much else is uncertain or unexplained, this is ample comfort to the weary heart.

I. The DEFINITION.

I once heard the late ALEXANDER STEWART say: "There are two things we wish to know about our dear departed ones, They are these: "Where are they?" and "How does it fare with them?". And these are the two things clearly revealed: "They are with Christ" and "It is very far better" (Phil. 1. 23).

But there is much more made known to us as to the future than this; much is said of Heaven and Hereafter in the Scriptures that is refreshing and strengthening to meditate upon.

First as to

The Use of the Word

HEAVEN. It is found both in the singular and plural forms—Heaven or the Heavens. I doubt, from a study of the occurrences, if they are really to be distinguished in meaning.

The Heaven and the Heaven of Heavens cannot contain God (1 Kings 8. 27), yet we read, "God is in His temple, let all the earth keep silence before Him" (Hab. 2. 20).

Christ entered into Heaven itself, yet we read: "Your Master also is in the Heavens" (Eph. 6. 9), and the Thessalonians waited "for His Son from the Heavens" (1 Thess. 1. 10). Our conversation (citizenship), our better substance (Heb. 10. 34); our inheritance (1 Peter 1. 4); our treasure (Luke 12. 33); our reward (Matt. 5. 12); and your Father (Luke 11. 2); are all in the Heavens.

Matthew uses the word in all 84 times, only 25 times in the singular. Luke and John together (including Acts and Revelation) use the word almost always in the singular. Out of 136 uses, only once does John use the plural form (Rev. 12. 12), and Luke only six times. They may, therefore, be regarded as interchangeable terms.

The plural perhaps, sometimes, but not always, includes the three Heavens (2 Cor. 12. 2), the sky, the expanse or sidereal Heavens, and Heaven itself the abode of God.

The next question that arises is:

Is Heaven a Place?

or is it to be regarded as a sphere of Life and Being independent of place? No doubt the latter is the true thought, and that for the following reasons.

1. PLACES APART FROM CIRCUMSTANCES AND CONDITIONS cannot give any satisfaction. Any place without the Lord's presence would not be Heaven.

> "Could I be cast where Thou art not,
> That were indeed a dreadful lot;
> But regions none remote I call,
> Secure of finding God in all"   *(Guyon)*.

True, the Lord said, "I go to prepare a Place for you" (John 14. 2), and told us that in the Father's house are many mansions (the word is only used once elsewhere, and translated "abode," (John 14. 23); but the building or the site as we well know do not constitute the "Home." It is love makes the home, not the mansion or the cottage.

The child's definition of Heaven has never been surpassed. "Heaven is the place where everybody loves everybody." There may be, and no doubt are, wondrous places in which we shall live and move and have our being, but it is the *sphere* in which we move not the *place* that makes the Heaven.

2. THE LANGUAGE USED, though of places, is clearly intended of the sphere, rather than the physical position in which we live.

For example, we read in Hebrews 12. 22: "But we have come unto Mount Zion and unto the City of the Living God, the Heavenly Jerusalem and to an innumerable company of angels and to the general assembly and Church of the firstborn which are written in Heaven, and to God the Judge of all, and to the spirits of just men made perfect, and to Jesus the Meditator of the New Covenant, and to the Blood of sprinkling."

Here places are named—Mount Zion and the New Jerusalem the City of the Living God; but since we are said now to have come to them, they are evidently not to be regarded as physical positions, or material places, but as the sphere of Heavenly associations, to which we as believers have come in Christ.   It is the spiritual City, the Company, and the Covenant that form our joy and blessedness.   Both in Gal. 4. 26 and Rev. 21. 1 we have this same sphere of blessedness brought before us under the figure of a city and the name of Jerusalem.

What then is Heaven?

It may be said to consist in three things: (1) THE STATE; (2) THE SPHERE; and (3) The SOCIETY in which believers live and move and have their being after this life.

But this does not exhaust the inquiry, for we find that different *periods* are spoken of, and that our condition varies with these periods. They may be stated thus: (1) the period *immediately after death*, before the redemption of the body at the Coming of Christ. (2) The period *between the Coming of Christ and the creation of the New Heavens and the New Earth*. (3) The Eternal Ages.

II. **The STATE**.

This must be considered in a twofold way: (1) Our Physical State and (2) Our Moral and Spiritual State.

1. **Our Physical State**

after death varies with the different periods of our existence. There is a period spoken of as the *Adoption*, that is to say, the Redemption of the Body (Rom. 8. 23). This is said to be our hope which yet we see not, but patiently wait for.

This time is evidently the Coming of Christ. It is described in 1 Cor. 15. 23-58. It is the First Resurrection, when those who are Christ's (23) rise to meet Him in the clouds at His Coming in the air, as described in 1 Thess. 4. 15-18.

Then the body is raised and changed. The mortal (those living at His Coming) put on immortality and the corruptible (those in the graves) put on incorruption. The body they receive, though the same in continuity and identity, being that sown in corruption, dishonour, and weakness, is raised a spiritual body (44) in incorruption, glory, and power (43) It is given "a body as it hath pleased Him" (38), and these bodies will vary in glory (41. 42).

In Phil. 3. 21 we are told that the Lord at His Coming will change our body of humiliation and fashion it like unto His glorious body.

Until that Day we are in a disembodied state. In 2 Cor. 5. 1-5 we learn that the physical body, "our earthly house of this tabernacle," dissolves (a perfect description of the decomposition of a dead body); but that there is a "building from God," a house not made with hands, eternal and from Heaven, with which we shall be "clothed upon," and then mortality will be swallowed up in life (4). Then we shall sing the triumph song of Hosea 13. 14 and 1 Cor. 15. 55.

Is Paradise Part of Hades?

It has sometimes been affirmed that at death the believer passes to be with the Lord in Paradise, and that Paradise is part of Hades (in the O.T. Sheol), the abode of the dead.

I can, however, find no justification for saying that Paradise is part of Hades. There are serious objections to such a suggestion.

(1) It would, of course, mean that *Our Lord is still in Hades*, which is certainly not true (Heb. 9. 24), for the saints pass to be with

the Lord in His actual presence (Phil. 1. 23; 2 Cor. 5. 8).

(2) *Hades is always spoken of as down*, whereas Paul was caught up into Paradise.

(3) *Paradise is identified with the third Heaven* in 2 Cor. 12. 2-4, "I knew a man . . . caught up to the third Heaven . . . such a man caught up to Paradise."

(4) In the incident of the rich man and Lazarus, we are distinctly told there is a great and impassable gulf *fixed between Abraham's bosom and Hades*.

(5) *The Tree of Life is in the midst of the Paradise of God* (Rev. 2. 7). This we can hardly believe to be in Hades.

(6) The only other reference to Paradise is *the case of the dying thief* (Luke 23. 43). Can we believe that his soul was left in Hades? How then could he be with his Lord, whose soul was not so left? (Acts 2. 31).

2. **Our Moral and Spiritual State**.

It is obvious that there is no Heaven for an evil man. The unregenerate could not breathe in the atmosphere of Heaven. "Except a man be born again he cannot see the Kingdom of God" (John 3. 3); except he be converted he shall not enter it (Matt. 18. 3). Heaven is certainly a *prepared place for a prepared people*.

Is a vile, wicked-living man, who has hated everything of God, and lived as far from holiness of life as can be conceived, to be suddenly introduced into a realm where all is of God and perfect in holiness? Would he care for it? Could he live in it? No; no more than a fish taken from the depths of the sea could live in the pure light and beauty of the sunshine above. He would be out of his element, and all around him contrary to every instinct of his fallen nature. He would perish.

What then is Heaven?

Heaven then consists first of all in a *state of conformity to the likeness of Christ*. What a man is, determines both his happiness and usefulness. Bliss lies not in surroundings, but in state. Perfect love is perfect delight. Perfect power, to appeciate good and beauty and holiness is perfect enjoyment Perfect and sinless activity is perfect usefulness. Perfect obedience is perfect joy. No words describe Heaven better than these: "We shall be like Him, for we shall see Him as He is" (1 John 3. 2).

To this we have been predestinated (Rom. 8. 29) to be holy as He is holy (Eph. 1. 4). This the Psalmist looked forward to as his real joy. "I shall be satisfied when I awake with Thy likeness" (Psa. 17. 15).

Heaven is not, as a foolish novelist has stated, a big bribe—Be good and you shall go to a city of gold. No, it is the joy of the soul to look for this, to be like Him—changed into the same image.

The expressions used in the 8th chapter of Romans are remarkable, and repay earnest meditation, but they all point this way. We are to be glorified together (17), glory is to be revealed in us (18), the sons of God are to be manifested (19) and to pass from the bondage of corruption to the liberty of the glory of the children of God (21). They are in short to be conformed to the image of His Son. He will then be the firstborn among the brethren—all bearing His likeness, all meet companions for Him through eternity. Can any Heaven be conceived better than this?

III. The SPHERE.

The believer, at his conversion to God, is introduced into a new sphere of life. It is known as "the Heavenlies." It may be fairly regarded as an anticipation on earth of the joys of Heaven.

The five references to the Heavenlies in Ephesians reveal the nature of this new sphere of living and activity into which we have been brought in Christ.

1. It is

The Sphere of all Spiritual Blessings

(Eph. 1. 3). Spiritual blessing cannot be enjoyed in a carnal or worldly atmosphere. As Spurgeon once said of theatre-going Christians, "I might as well expect to grow prize roses in my coal cellar as develop spiritual life in such surroundings."

It is only as we walk in Christ and live in the Heavenly atmosphere that the blessings

found in Him are entered into an experience.
2. It is

The Sphere of Happy Association

and COMMUNION WITH CHRIST (Eph. 12. 26).
We are raised up and made to sit with Him in
the Heavenlies. The highest earthly experience
of spiritual life is found in this, and as we have
seen, it is to be continued to us in the ages
to come (7). He is above all rule and authority,
and we sit with Him.
3. It is

The Sphere in which Christ is Glorified

IN HIS SAINTS (Eph. 3. 10). The manifold
wisdom of God is to be displayed to the principalities and powers of the unseen world
through the Church. He is, we are told elsewhere, to be admired in His saints. It is so
now as they live in the Heavenlies, it will be
so in perfection in the ages to come.
4. It is

The Sphere of Victory

(Eph. 6. 2). Now we wrestle against mighty
foes. The world rulers of this darkness and
hosts of wicked spirits in the Heavenlies, but
as we live in that sphere we "have done (over-
come) all" (v. 13), and can stand fast and
persevere.

Heaven itself will find us in that Heavenly
sphere unopposed and in the full enjoyment of
that which we have here but tasted. But how

precious to our souls has been that foretaste.

To be blessed by Him, to be seated with Him; for Him to be glorified in us, and to share with Him His perfect and complete triumph—this will be Heaven. The transfer from the Heavenlies (the foretaste) to Heaven (the consummation). Ours it is now to anticipate the bliss by living, walking, and serving in Christ in the Heavenlies.

IV. **The SOCIETY.**

No small part of Heaven will be the company we enjoy.

WE ARE COME TO IT NOW! Just as we are in the Heavenlies now. Then we shall enjoy it unhindered through Eternity. "We are come to Mount Zion," that is the seat of royalty and rule of David.

> "Zion, thrice happy place!
> There David's greater Son
> Hath fixed His royal throne;
> He sits in grace and judgment there."

We are come to the City of the Living God, the Heavenly Jerusalem, that is, the metropolis that will be the centre of His rule in the regenerated earth and Heavens.

We see Him now crowned with glory and honour, but He waits at present till His enemies (and ours) be made His footstool (Heb. 10. 13). Then He shall reign, and we shall reign with Him. Of which more later.

We are come to Myriads. The hosts of angels; the General Assembly and Church of the First-

2

born enrolled in Heaven; to God, Judge of all;
the spirits of just men perfected, and to Jesus
and His precious sprinkled blood.   What
company is ours! Now in some small measure,
then in full and perfect delight.   To pass over
to the other side, beyond the veil that hides
it all from our eyes (except the eyes of faith),
to see the King in His beauty, to be with Him
and among this glorious company in that
holy realm—this is Heaven.

V. **The SERVICE**.

But Heaven is

A Sphere of Service.

"His servants shall serve Him" (Rev. 22. 3).
Heaven is our rest—but not the rest of in-
activity, but of perfect satisfaction.   The rest
of the warrior who puts his armour off and
returns to home and the peace of mutual love
and felicity with those who are dearest.

For the Church triumphant awaits us there.
Our loved who have passed on before.   We
shall know as we are known.   We shall "go
to them" (2 Sam. 12. 23), and to the spirits
of just men made perfect.

The Subject of Service

introduces a difficult question.   What is the
nature of that service, and where is the sphere
of it?

The answer appears from many Scriptures
to be that the saints will share with their

Lord in the administration of the Kingdom, which He will establish and which is spoken of as "the Kingdom of Heaven" (of the Heavens) "the Kingdom of God," and "the Kingdom of His dear Son," which ultimately will embrace the whole creation.

Whether any part of that service is on earth, it is unnecessary to inquire, for the New Heavens and the New Earth are always spoken of together, which seems to imply that they will no longer be separated arbitrarily as they are now to us in the flesh, but will form one sphere of life and service.

Nor are we able to distinguish the different periods. Possibly until we receive the new spiritual body we shall rest, expecting with the saints still on earth, and looking for that Coming of the Lord for His saints—the adoption—when He will usher in the Day of the Lord and establish His throne of righteousness.

1. *The Saints will have their share in the Judgment apparently.* "Do ye know that the saints shall judge the world? . . . Know ye not that we shall judge angels?" (1 Cor. 6. 2, 3). A special part being reserved for the twelve apostles, "Verily, I say unto you, that ye which have followed Me, in the regeneration, when the Son of Man shall sit in the Throne of His glory, ye also shall sit upon twelve thrones judging the twelve tribes of Israel" (Matt. 19. 28).

2. *They will have Rule according to their*

Faithful service down here. This we learn from the parables of our Lord. "His Lord said unto him, Well done, thou good and faithful servant, thou hast been faithful over a few things, I will make thee ruler over many things; enter thou into the joy of thy Lord" (Matt. 25. 21). "And He said unto him, Well, thou good servant: because thou hast been faithful in a very little, have thou authority over ten cities" (Luke 19. 17).

We are unable to say much more than this, probably the state of things there is indescribable in human language. When Paul was caught up to the third Heaven, into Paradise, He heard "unspeakable words which it is not lawful for men to utter."

How this quickens our appetite and leaves us in awe-struck wonder at those things hereafter to be revealed, the glory to which we are called.

The Scriptures end with the magnificent description of

The New Heaven and the New Earth

(Rev. 21. 1). It is no doubt meant to be a consummation of all that has gone before, the grand climax. It's glowing, figurative language raises a thousand unanswered questions that curiosity would like to ask, but which faith is content to leave unanswered.

Some things, however, seem clear:

1. *In those New Heavens and New Earth the beautiful things of the present creation find a*

place—only more beautiful and purged from the curse upon the ground we read of in Gen. 3. 17-19. The river, the trees, the garden (Paradise) the fruit; these suggest that those material things which have given us such delight in this life, will be there too, for us to rejoice in them. Not a few Scriptures suggest that the animal creation, often so beloved of men, will be there in harmless and happy life (Isa. 65. 17-25; 66. 22).

2. *That the New Jerusalem will be the Metropolis of the regenerated earth,* in which the nations of those which are saved walk, and the kings of the earth do bring their glory and honor into it.

3. *That then the Lord will Himself dwell among them* and be their light and glory, for the name of the city shall be Jehovah Shammah (the Lord is there).

To sum up, Heaven is best described in the fourfold promises: WE SHALL SEE HIM; BE FOR EVER WITH HIM; BE LIKE HIM, AND SERVE HIM.

CHAPTER II

What Heaven Means to Me

By J. B. WATSON, London

I THINK of Heaven as

The Place of Ideal Government

and order.   John of Patmos, when a door was opened to him in Heaven, saw first of all—a throne.   Heaven is the sphere of perfect rule, and therefore of harmonious blessedness and abiding security.   "Thy will be done on earth as it is in Heaven" (Matt. 6. 10), is one of the petitions of the Disciples' Prayer, intimating that Heaven is the place where the will of God is the universal law.   Heaven is blessed both in the benignity of its ever-blessed Ruler, and in the heart obedience rendered to Him by every dweller in that serene abode.

"I go, " said RICHARD HOOKER, as he neared the gates of the City, "to *a world of order.*" The blessedness of Heaven to the author of "Ecclesiastical Polity" was its sublime perfection of government.

I think of Heaven as

The Home of the Soul

Our Lord called it "the Father's House" (John 14. 2), and a father's house is also a children's home. "Home" is one of the tenderest words in our English tongue. Every true heart turns towards home when the day's task is through. As the needle is drawn towards the Pole, so are our hearts drawn homeward as the night falls. Kindred souls are there; those who love us, understand us, our kin who delight to serve us and do to us good.

From battling with the hard forces of an unfeeling world, what balm to the mind there is in fireside converse with our dearest-on-earth circle! So when the din and dust of life's day is through, Heaven waits to welcome the believer. "At Home with the Lord" (2 Cor. 5. 8), is the peace, if not the glory of Heaven.

"I feel like a schoolboy bounding for home," said the war-scarred champion of a hundred fights for Christ in dark Burma, ADONIRAM JUDSON, as he drew near the moment to doff his harness.

I think of Heaven as

The Place of Perfect Fitness.

RICHARD BAXTER, author of "The Saints' Everlasting Rest," faithful among the faithful, and most diligent of pastors, as his frame weakened during his last illness, whispered in response to an inquiry as to how he felt, "I am almost well." For Heaven will be the saints' everlasting rest indeed!

There we shall not longer be humiliated by our bodies. They shall not then impose their severe limitations upon our ability to serve the

Lord, nor continually thwart the activities of our ransomed spirits. Nay, but the body, sharing in the glorious Redemption Christ obtained for us, shall be the suited vessel through which our souls shall express themselves.

> "There all is new, and never shall be old.
> For time is not, nor age, nor slow decay;
> No dying eyes, no heart grown strange and cold,
> All pain, all death, all sighing fled away."

I think of Heaven as

The Place of Enlarged Service.

"His servants shall *serve* Him" (Rev. 22. 3). It follows that it must be so, since Heaven is where His will is fully done.

The only satisfying explanation of the discipline of our present condition is that it is God's training of the future administrators and executors of His eternal purposes.

"Rule thou over ten cities" (Luke 19. 19) was the word to the faithful servant who had developed his character and capacity amid the opportunities of the present life. And if it be said that the reward of rule over ten, or five, cities is Millennial, the question immediately arises: Is then the blessed service of the Thousand Years to be succeeded by an eternal inertia? Nay, verily,

> "For doubt not but that in the realms above
> There are yet other offices of love,
> That other ministries of joy there are,
> For it is written that His servants there
> Shall serve Him still."

I think of Heaven as

The Place of Unhindered Worship.

Here we gather in twos and threes, amid much brokenness, aversion, and weakness. The feebleness of our praise is painfully obvious. We could not hope for its acceptance save for our Great High Priest. The heart lags, the mind is dull, memory is weak, and the distractions of our earthly lot obtrude unasked upon our holiest moments. The very exercises we engage in when met for worship sometimes come between us and the Lord. Jarring notes spoil the praise, coldness of spirit chills the thanksgiving. Too often, alas, we come before the Lord empty. It is only His matchless grace that encourages us to know our poor worship is accepted.

But Yonder, how different! What praise! What glorious unison of full-hearted, pure, untainted and unceasing worship!

> "The countless multitudes on high,
> That tune their song to Jesus' Name,
> All merit of their own deny,
> And Jesus' worth alone proclaim."

Says JOHN BUNYAN of that fair land, "Now, just as the gates were opened to let in the men, I looked in after them, and behold, the City shone like the sun: the streets also were paved with gold, and in them walked many men with crowns on their heads, palms in their hands, and golden harps to play withal. There were also of them that had wings, and they answered one another without intermission, saying, Holy, Holy, Holy is the Lord . . . Which when I had seen I wished myself among them. "

I think of Heaven as

The Place of Open Vision

of the Glorious Christ.   Here we have walked by faith, the inward vision of the soul.   Then shall glory-vision be ours; we shall gaze direct upon the Lord Jesus Christ.   Dimly now we trace but dark outlines of Heavenly things, seeing "through a mirror in an enigma, but then face to face" (1 Cor. 13. 12).

What intellectual enlargement awaits the saints in the land where we shall know even as we have been known!   But, better, than all increase of knowledge, dearer than all advance of capacity, more precious than all perfection of adaptation to environment, will be this simple, satisfying, longed-for consummation. "THEY SHALL SEE HIS FACE" (Rev. 22. 4).

Said SAMUEL RUTHERFORD joyfully from his Aberdeen prison: "The Lamb is all the glory of Immanuel's Land. "

"The Man of Sychar!   Oh, I shall see the Man of Sychar's Well!" cried J. G. BELLETT as the shadows of this present world thinned, and the rays of the glory-light of Heaven began to filter through to his Home-going soul.

BUT DIMLY WE DISCERN THE GLORIES THAT AWAIT US.   "It doth not yet appear what we shall be" (1 John 3. 2).   There is a grave reticence in Holy Writ on this theme.   But there

is one central, final, and settling fact clearly
revealed, which puts the key of Heaven into
the hand of the least instructed believer:
"Christ is Heaven's All-in-All, and we shall
be *'with Him'* there."

> "My knowledge of that life is small,
>   The eye of faith is dim;
> It is enough that Christ knows all,
>   And I shall be *with Him*!"

CHAPTER III

Some Scriptural Particulars

By FRANKLIN FERGUSON, Palmerston, N.Z.

WHEN a person contemplates visiting another country for the first time, the
mind gets full of it, and all available information is eagerly sought after; and the visit becomes the chief topic of conversation, with
the very interesting sights you expect to see,
and the pleasures to be enjoyed shortly.

We are going to a Country surpassing for
glory and beauty the utmost stretch of our
imagination—Heaven.   Concerning it we often
sing:

"Heaven is my Fatherland,
Heaven is my Home."

Through infinite grace we have become the
Children of God, redeemed by the "Precious
Blood of Christ" (1 Pet. 1. 18, 19), and can
look up to Heaven to the One who fills the
Throne, and say, Father! We are going to a
land "that is fairer than day," with the sweet
thought that it is *Home*.

Yet, strange it is, how seldom we have
heard an address, or read an article on Heaven.
Perhaps this earth engages our attention out

of all proportion, so that we are not declaring, as we should, that we "seek a Country" (Heb. 11. 13-16).

There are Three Heavens.

(1) The Heaven of the clouds, the rain and the lightning; (2) the Heaven of the sun, the moon, and the stars; and (3) the "Heaven of Heavens," or "third Heaven" as it is called (2 Cor. 12. 2).

The latter is the abode of God, the angels, and the church. The distance there must be infinitely great. Astronomy can penetrate and measure the vast spaces of the starry Heavens, but no telescope can locate the dwelling of our God, and the place of His throne.

HOW LONG WILL IT TAKE TO GO THERE? seeing that astronomers tell us that light has been hundreds of thousands of years in reaching this earth from certain stars? We reply in the words of Scripture, "Absent from the body, present with the Lord" (2 Cor. 5. 8); the inference being that the interval between leaving the body and being with Christ is of the briefest duration.

How this incredibly quick passage can be, forms no part of revelation; but faith accepts it as one of the great wonders of our Almighty God and Father. We already know that a sound can go round the world in a fraction of time; but there are hidden secrets of travel yet withheld from the knowledge of Man.

What is Heaven?

It is a place, literally (John 14. 2), not simply a condition, though it will be certainly ecstatic. It is a Place to which our Lord has gone, and He calls it His Father's "House," where there are many "Mansions," or abiding places. Yonder He has prepared a "place" for us, and if it were not so He would have told us.

THERE IS A PARADISE (2 Cor. 12. 4). God made a Paradise for our first parents—a specially beautiful spot in the midst of a creation fresh from His hand; there He walked and talked with Adam and Eve until sin was committed.

What a charming "garden of delights" it must have been! It has gone from this scene; yet there is another in the realms above, where you and I, sinners saved by the Blood of the Lamb, will "eat of the Tree of Life, which is in the midst of the Paradise of God" (Rev. 2. 7), where no sin can enter, nor the communion be hindred. How gladsome is the prospect!

HEAVEN IS A COUNTRY (Heb. 11. 14-16), as truly a country as any on earth, but transcending all human conception. How beautiful has God made this earth, with its magnificently varied scenery; still wonderfully lovely notwithstanding the fall of man. If this earthly scene has such charm, then what will the Heavenly be like, as our eyes behold the "better country," where, indeed, "every prospect pleases" and man no longer is vile, and God and the Lamb are there.

THERE ARE INHERITANCES IN HEAVEN (1 Pet. 1. 4), which will be as truly possessed and enjoyed, as ever Israel of old did in the Land of Promise. Likewise there are many REWARDS (1 Cor. 2. 14) for faithful service. We know how a country will honour its illustrious citizens; even thus will it be with those whom the King Eternal delights to honour—honour surpassing all earthly glory (compare Esther 6. 7-9).

The Conditions of Heaven

will differ greatly from our present experiences. For instance, there will be no night there, but one eternal glorious day; no sun or moon will shine, for God Himself will lighten all the fair scene; the inhabitants will feel no fatigue, and they never grow old, and they count not time by years; nor shall sorrow, pain, tears, or death be known any more at all, for God will wipe away all tears and make all things new.

WE SHALL NEITHER BE ANGELS OR SPIRITS IN HEAVEN, but shall have bodies just like our Lord's resurrection body, and that body could be handled (Phil. 3. 21; Luke 24. 39). Our present mortal bodies will undergo the needful "change" to enable them to bear the "eternal weight of glory" to come.

There will be singing and music in Heaven (Rev. 5. 9; 14. 2), which can only be thought of as *rapturous*.

THERE ARE SWEET GLIMPSES OF HEAVEN given us in the Word, in wonderfully descriptive language, which strangely moves us at times, and sets the heart longing for the Day when the eyes shall at last behold our beautiful and everlasting Home. And the best of all is that our Lord Jesus Christ will welcome us there, who loved us and gave Himself for us, and so shall we ever be with Him.

CHAPTER IV

Heaven in Comparison with the Universe

By A. C. ROSE, India

HEAVEN is one of the words most frequently used by Christians. The Scriptures are full of references to it.

Where is Heaven?

It is easy to answer generally, "Where God
is," but it is possible to give more detailed
answers. For instance it is "above." The
Lord Jesus said, "I am from above." He
"came down from Heaven" (John 6. 38).
God "looks down," and some day we shall be
"caught up" (1 Thess. 4. 17). Heaven is God's
dwelling place, and the earth is His footstool.
The ascending Lord went *up* on His way Home
to prepare a Place for us.

It is true that Heaven and the Heaven of
heavens cannot contain the Eternal God so
that He dwells in humble and contrite hearts,
but these are the outposts of His Empire, His
throne is established in Heaven, and the
Heavens do rule.

The Universe and Heaven.

The modern mind is greatly occupied with
the dimensions of the universe. Telescopes

3

reveal the almost infinite fields of space, sown with worlds. We are told there are as many stars in the sky as there are grains of sand upon all the seashores of the world. Long ago the Scripture spoke in the same terms of sand and stars. We are told amazing things about the size and composition of other worlds, so that the mind reels in an attempt to comprehend a globe 180,000 miles in diameter.

Allowing the necessary margin for human error and the effect of unknown factors, we believe that when we look up into the starry skies we are actually looking into the Heavens. Somewhere, there, are the many Mansions and the hosts of the Redeemer who have crossed the flood, and the shining ranks of angel legions.

"And when the strife is fierce, the warfare long,
Steals on the ear the distant triumph song,
And hearts are brave again, and arms are strong.
Alleluia!"

The Stars and Heaven.

It is said that none of the stars can possibly support life owing to the tremendous temperatures existing. This is nonsense. Human life as we experience it is not standard. The standard is that other, eternal life, which is not to be regarded in terms of temperatures. Heat and light are variations of the same phenomenon, and we know that the King of kings dwells in light unapproachable.

It is probable that our thoughts of Heaven are too materialistic. The life to come is intensely spiritual. The language of the Apocalypse is the graphic language of parable, using earthly shadows to teach Heavenly substance. We shall err if we expect the substance to be limited by the shadows.

The Nursery of Heaven.

Therefore, far from allowing the vastness of the universe to overwhelm us with a sense of our own insignificance, we look up past creation, to a faithful Creator, and we say, "Abba, Father!" We bow in adoration before Him because of His so great love to one of the least of His worlds, destined to be eternally famous as the birthplace of His Son and the nursery of Heaven.

What is Heaven?

We have seen that there is ample room in the universe for such a place. There, we believe, the spirits of believers find their place of rest. Released from the swaddling bands of the body, they are "with Christ, which is very far better" than any earthly best—even the Lord's table. There the servants of God serve Him perfectly, there His children love Him perfectly, there His priests worship Him perfectly. Every problem is solved, every question is answered, every fear is wiped, and "God is all and in all" (1 Cor. 15. 28).

Three Things in Heaven.

True, it is the place of JUDGMENT; but not of condemnation, for Christians. Let us not shrink from this, but rather look forward to the final test of fire and the revelation of every secret thing. But what about that——! and that——? Well, it will be settled once and for all, and *grace* will be given even to suffer loss.

Heaven is the place of SONG. Music will be restored to its rightful place as the expression of worship, and every ear and voice will be tuned. It is the place of FELLOWSHIP. Shall we know one another there? Surely we are to "know as we are known" (1 Cor. 13. 12). It would be ignorance not to know. We are to see our Lord, and to be "like Him," but that does not mean we shall lose our personality. The likenesss is that with which the child resembles his parent. All that constitutes life here is but the type of the life eternal. These are kindergarten days of preparation for Heavenly responsibilities.

The Infinity of Our Home.

Resurrection will equip us with spiritual bodies suited to our new environment. The limitations of our earthly being will have gone. There will be infinite capacity for joy and love.

"Ah! think! to step on shore and that shore Heaven
 That where He is there we too shall be!
 To see His face who never failed us here,
 Whose blood washed all our crimson sins away;
 To pass from pain and sorrow to His own side,
 And there for ever, ever to abide!"

When is it? "Absent . . . present." What could be more simple. "To wake up and find it glory!" This is not to say that we at once enter upon all our new experiences. It is probable that many of these await the last act of redemption when we shall be clothed with celestial bodies. But we shall be at Home immediately with angels for our servants. Now they wait upon us, unwearied, invisible; then we shall see them in their beauty and thank them for their guardian care. There is but a step between us and Glory. The veil is thin, the time is short, it behoves us to be men of the girt loin and burning lamp. If He comes what joy to cheat old death! If not the utmost that can happen is a last wrestle with a well-known enemy, and then the victor's song:

> "For Zion is our Home:
>   Jerusalem, the city of our God.
>   O happy Home! O happy children there!
>   O blissful mansions of our Father's house!
>   O walks surpassing Eden to delight:
> Here are the harvests reaped once sown in tears:
> Here is the banquet of the wine of heaven,
> Riches of glory incorruptible,
> Crowns, amaranthine crowns of victory,
> The voice of harpers harping with their harps,
> The anthem of the holy Cherubim,
> The crystal river of the Spirit's joy,
> The Bridal palace of the Prince of Peace,
> The Holiest of Holies—God is here."

CHAPTER V

Our Eternal Home

By ROBERT LEE, Manchester

"HALF an hour in Heaven, and I am ready for anything," was the testimony of a poor working man. He meant much more than merely having a heavenly time in public worship or private devotion, though naturally that is a good preparation for the walk of life. He meant meditating on Heaven, yea, visiting that blessed abode in heart and mind; but more even than that—for we are *living in Heaven*. That is true of us *positionally*, as Ephesians 1. 3 and 2. 6 declare; that is also true of us *experimentally*, as Matthew 6. 21 shows. Christ, our best beloved, our heart's treasure, is there, and therefore in consequence we are there.

Fifty years ago, our fathers dwelt much on this subject—so much so that many began to think that the sole, or primary object of our Redeemer was to take us to Heaven. Have we not gone to the other extreme? The Gospel prepares us to live; and because prepared to live we are prepared to die. "Let me die the death of the righteous, and let my last end be like His" (Num. 23. 10), was the prophet

Balaam's desire, yet not granted, because he was not prepared to live the life of the righteous.

To meditate on Heaven should be no difficult task for the believer, because with saintly Samuel Rutherford he can say, "Christ hath come and run away with my heart and love, so that neither heart nor love is mine."

D. L. Moody told of a man he knew who lost his only child, and the sorrow almost broke his heart. He had never given much serious thought to a future life, but after his child was taken, his friends were surprised to find him continually studying that sacred Book, the Bible. Someone asked him the reason, and he said he was trying to find out about the place where his boy had gone. We all have lost many loved ones who, because believers, have most assuredly gone to Heaven—strange, if we do not take up the Bible to find out what it has to say about that Blessed Abode!

There is a third reason why many of us should be interested in Heaven, and that is because in our case old age is creeping on, and if the Lord tarries, in the ordinary course of things, we shall soon be called up there to higher service.

In wonderful wisdom our gracious Master has given us information on important matters in simple language. For example, there is not a finer summary of His personal Premillennial Advent, than in Acts 1. 11. It seems incapable of misunderstanding. The same is true regarding Heaven. For surely language could not be simpler, nor more graphic, than we have in John 14. 2: "In My Father's House are many mansions," or as another version, "many resting places." "In My Father's House"—"HOME!" What an attractive decription of Heaven! Heaven is our Eternal Home.

1. **Heaven is a Homely Place**.

Mark you, a *place*—not a mere state, though it is that. Of what value is a state without a place? A right state is a preparation for the right place. As to its exact locality, we know it is in the third Heaven (2 Cor. 12. 2). The meaning of "the bands of Orion" (Job 38. 31) was unknown until the modern telescope revealed what is known as "the open space in Orion," a great spiral nebula in the belt of Orion in the shape of a band or ring. This band is estimated to be fifty trillion miles in depth, and twenty trillion miles in width. It is by far the most glorious scene in the Heavens, and seems like a gateway into the Heaven of Heavens, with the glory from the Throne of Jehovah shining through.

Heaven is a homely place,

Not a Place of Weariness and Dreariness!

Home—what a mystic name; it conjures up visions of peace, joy, delight, happy fellowship, love. Though some of us now have homes of our own, yet longingly and lovingly we think of the olden days when we gathered together in our earthly homes with mother and father, long since gone home. Heaven, a home! Ah, that tones down the feeling of awfulness in the thought of the glorious beyond. HOME ah, that is just what Heaven is! Amidst the august and unimaginable glories of Heaven, the old feeling will come back again of being little children, nestling safe in the Father's Home. Yes, Heaven is a homely place!

II. Heaven is a Home of Adoring Worship.

Only on one other occasion beside this, so far as the Scriptures are concerned, did our Lord use the expression "House": "Make not My Father's House an house of merchandise" (John 2. 16). Thus our great future Home, will be the full realisation of what the earthly Temple was but the dim prophecy and shadow. Most of us lament here our human limitations which make our private and public devotions so poor and uninspiring. Even believers with a rich vocabulary, and a wonderful choice of ready and apt speech, are the first to confess how utterly unable at times they find themselves to be able adequately to express the deepest feelings of their hearts and spirits. Thank God, in the Day to come, those human limitations will be abolished, and all that will be a thing of the past, for then we shall worship as we ought. Our Heavenly life will be a life of praise.

III. Heaven is a Home Without a Shadow.

This certainly is a big difference to the very best of earthly homes. Is there one earthly home without a shadow? What dark shadows throw their gruesome shapes across most homes. Some have "skeletons in the cupboard"—a weird and awesome saying. Yet our Heavenly Home is a Home without a shadow.

THE SHADOW OF SIN. There is not an earthly home, however good, but sin at times casts its shadow over it. Yet what is the meaning of this? "And there shall in no wise enter into it anything that defileth, neither whatsoever worketh abomination or maketh a lie" (Rev. 21. 27). Once sin cast its awful shadow over Heaven, when that bright cherubim, Satan, led that awful revolt which culminated in his and his followers' utter ruin. Is that why the Scriptures speak of Heaven as requiring cleansing? (Heb. 9. 23). But that shadow has gone for ever. Sin, therefore, now will never cast its horrible and defiling shadow over our Heavenly Home.

THE SHADOW OF SORROW. It is a home without a shadow of sorrow: "God shall wipe away all tears from their eyes; and there shall be no more death, neither sorrow, nor crying, neither shall there be any more pain" (Rev. 21. 4). Shadow of death—what a saddening shadow this is! Yet that shadow will have gone for ever, for, listen, let us again repeat it: "There shall be no more death, neither sorrow, nor crying." Heaven will be a life of wonderful joy, and of entire absence of sorrow.

THE SHADOW OF REMOVAL. Some of us know what it is to be so attached to an earthly house that it has pained us to remove from that one into another. Yet that sorrow will for ever have gone when we reach up There, for it is written: "For here have we *no continuing* city, but we seek one to come" (Heb. 13. 14).

THE SHADOW OF SEPARATION. A fisher-woman who had lost her husband and two sons at sea off the Northumberland coast, was asked what she most liked to think about in Heaven, and without hesitation she replied: "And there shall be no more sea." To her, the sea had been cruel, and she loved to think of the Better Land as sealess, that is no separation, for here it is the seas and the oceans that separate those of one land from another. No shadow of separation there!

THE SHADOW OF NEED. In these days of world-wide financial depression, the old saying, "Keeping the wolf from the door," has a new significance; but up Yonder there will not be any shadow of need, for it is written: "They shall hunger no more, neither thirst any more: for the Lamb which is in the midst of the Throne, shall feed them and lead them into living Fountains of Water" (Rev. 7. 16, 17).

THE SHADOW OF NIGHT. For some, night has fears, and sometimes terrors. It is written: "And there shall be no night there, and they

need not candle neither the light of the sun";
therefore it will be a home of wonderful light.
This means, of course, that our immortal
bodies will be constructed very differently
from our present ones.

THE SHADOW OF WEARINESS. To the en-
thusiastic worker for God, sickness or weariness
of body which limits or arrests service is a
trying shadow. Heaven will know of no such
weariness. Our new bodies and ourselves will
not be capable of weariness, will need no
repose.

IV. Heaven is a Home of Blessed Reunion.

"Will we know one another in Heaven?"
inquired a worker's wife of her learned husband. "Why, of course we shall," he replied.
"We know one another here, and surely you
do not imagine that we shall be bigger fools
up there than we are here." The reply, though
rather rugged and uncouth, was sound common
sense. Certainly it would not be Heaven—
that truly human and blessed abode of which
Christ is the centre, if our individual person-
alities were annihilated, and we were unable
to recognise one another. Moses and Elijah
were recognised on the Mount of Transfigura-
tion, though dead or translated hundreds of
years. In that blessed spiritual world there
will still be distinctions of persons and per-
sonalities, with glorious possibilities of love
and fellowship. Heaven will be a life of un-

broken love. Reunion rests upon the permanence of personality. Personality is an eternal possession.

V. Heaven is a Home of Happy Service.

It would not be Heaven if it were not. We speak of some homes as "Hives of industry." Heaven is all that, for it is written: "And His servants shall *serve* Him" (Rev. 22. 3); "Therefore are they before the Throne of God and *serve* Him day and night." Of course, we are not informed of the kind of service that we shall be permitted to render. Heaven, therefore, is a life of doing; all being acts of worship. Most certainly it will be service without toil. There will be nothing laborious in the tasks that will be given to us, for the days of weariness and weakness will be for ever at an end. No doubt by eternal youth and vigour our bodies then will be able to accomplish all that we and the Lord will require. What a glorious thing that is—that death is not an end to the energies and activities which have here been consecrated to God.

VI. Heaven is a Spacious Home.

"In My Father's House are *many* Mansions," or "resting places." It is spacious, as well as beautiful. There will be ample room in the Father's house for all, with room enough to spare.

VII. **Heaven is a Home of Rest,**

though, as already noticed, a Home of happy
and blessed service.   "Many *resting* places"
is the Weymouth rendering of John 14. 2.
"Blessed are the dead which die in the Lord
from henceforth; yea, saith the Spirit that
they may *rest* from their labours" (Rev. 14.
13).   We have heard sick people say, "Oh,
I would give anything for rest!"   There, the
weary are at rest.   The life there will be a
restful one—none of the old weariness of the
heart or of the mind, or even of the body.
Our new body given at the Resurrection by
and by when Jesus Christ comes, will be
incapable of weariness.

VIII. **Heaven is a Home of Learning,**

that is, of ever increasing knowledge.   If this
were not so, then what is the meaning of John
17. 3, where our Lord distinctly declares that
Eternal life is given to us in order that we might
discover God, suggesting that the whole of
Eternity will be spent in getting to know God;
and then 1 Cor. 13. 12: "For now we see through
a glass, darkly; but then face to face: Now I
know in part; but then shall I know even as
also I am known. "   Language could not be
more definite—the Home we are going to will
be a home of learning, of ever-increasing
knowledge, for there our life will be one of
growth, without limit and without ceasing.
There, our life will never reach a point be-

yond which no advance is possible. Our knowledge will be perfect, and yet ever growing bigger and grander.

IX. **Heaven is a Home of Holy Laughter**.

JAMES CHALMERS, the great New Guinea missionary, heard a native Christian pray for help to live the holy, active life here for Christ, and hereafter "the place of laughter," for that was the meaning of the phrase he used. After a good day's work, and a good supper, the natives often sit in the street or platform, and shouts of laughter, screaming laughter may be heard, as story after story is told of the day's doings and sayings. All are happy and thoroughly enjoying themselves; and the native word for that custom was the word this native used to describe Heaven. Was he mistaken? No! Heaven will certainly be a home of Holy laughter. Our life's struggles will be over. We shall, with our perfect vision, and unbefogged minds, trace the Lord's guiding hand in our past. We shall tell our experiences, unravel His mysterious providences; and then, do not forget that Heaven is a place where thousands of little children are, and where children are there is laughter.

. . . .

There are two notable occurrences of the word "received" in John's Gospel (chaps. 14. 3; 1. 12). The Lord cannot receive us to that blessed Home on high if we, down here, do not receive Him into our hearts and lives.

"Christ possessed by faith here," said RUTHER-
FORD, "is young Heaven and glory in the bud."
But we cannot have the full flower without
the bud, neither can we have Heaven by and
by, if we have not Heaven here and now.
"The Lord will give grace and glory," was
the Psalmist's assurance. Notice, grace before
glory. But saith an old Divine, "Who chides
the servant for taking away the first course
at a feast, when the second consists of far
greater delicacies?" The Christian's first
course is GRACE, the second, GLORY. No
glory without grace.

CHAPTER VI

Heaven and its Eternal Blessings

By R. G. LORD, Ipswich

OUR information on this subject can only come from God through His Word, which gives us gleams of light on the subject such as we are capable of receiving in this present state, for we know but in part now (1 Cor. 13), and know nothing yet as we ought to know (1 Cor. 8. 2); and mere idle curiosity remains, as always, ungratified. First, then, we ask the the question:

I. WHAT IS HEAVEN?

While many may regard it as a mere state of existence, it seems clear that, just as Hell is the place of the lost dead, to be later consigned to the Lake of Fire, Heaven is a *real place* also, for

1. It is the Habitation of God the Father.

"Look down from Heaven and behold from the habitation of Thy holiness and of Thy glory" (Isa. 63. 15). "Hear Thou in Heaven Thy dwelling place" (1 Kings 8. 30, 39, 43, 49). "If I ascend up into Heaven, Thou art there" (Psa. 139. 8). "One is your Father which is in Heaven" (Matt. 23. 9).

4

2. It is the Home of God the Son, the Lord Jesus Christ.

"No man hath ascended up to Heaven but He that came down from Heaven, even the Son of Man which is in Heaven" (John 3. 13). Whether the Lord Jesus Himself spoke these words, or they form an explanation given by John, as some believe, in no wise affects the truth of our proposition; in either case, they are words of the Holy Ghost. Again, in John 6. 38 the Lord Jesus states: "I came down from Heaven, not to do Mine own will, but the will of Him that sent Me. "

Whither He has returned. A host of Scriptures attest this fact. Perhaps the following will suffice as proof: "So then after the Lord had spoken unto them, He was received up into Heaven, and sat on the right hand of God" (Mark 16. 19). "Whom the heavens must receive until the times of restitution of all things" (Acts 3. 21. See also Acts 2. 34; Eph. 4. 10; 1 Peter 3. 22; John 20. 17, etc.).

Whence He will come again. Paul appeals to the Philippian saints to walk as having him as an example, "For, " says he, "our conversation is in Heaven, from whence also we look for the Saviour, the Lord Jesus Christ" (Phil. 3. 20), and the Thessalonian saints "turned to God from idols to serve the living and true God, and wait for His Son from Heaven" (1 Thess. 1. 10), for "the Lord Himself shall descend from Heaven with a shout, " etc. (1 Thess. 4. 16).

3. **It is the Home of God the Holy Ghost**.

For John (the Baptist) bare record, saying, "I saw the Spirit descending from Heaven like a dove" (John 1. 32). And on that memorable Day of Pentecost, "there came a sound from Heaven . . . and they were all filled with the Holy Ghost" (Acts 2. 2, 4); and "with the Holy Ghost sent down from Heaven, was preached the Gospel" to those whom Peter wrote in 1 Pet. 1. 12.

4. **It is the Home of the Living Creatures and of myriads of Holy, unfallen angels** (Rev. 4. 5).

"Beasts" is a somewhat unfortunate translation in the A.V., and the "living creatures" of the R.V., and other versions also, is preferable. They are possibly the same as the cherubim and seraphim. John tells us that the number of angels he beheld around the Throne in Heaven (Rev. 5. 11) was one hundred million and millions besides! Blessed spirits, thus to be employed about the Throne, and still more blessed the ransomed Church of God to be on the Throne in union and association with its Risen Lord! And sad it is to think of the fallen angels revolted through and along with Satan, who ruined the third part of those created (Rev. 12. 4, 7, 9), created for the glory of God, to be His ministers and do His pleasure (Psa. 103. 21), which in eternal ages past they did, until corrupted by the fallen arch-enemy of God and man,

5. **It is the Eternal Home of the Re-deemed of all ages**.

We take it that from righteous Abel (Matt. 23. 35) onwards, all along the line of faith, to the last soul saved by grace from this old sin-ruined world at the end of time will find their place in the glorious Heavenly Home above. Abraham, Isaac, Jacob, and others all died in faith, having confessed themselves as strangers and pilgrims on the earth (Heb. 11. 13), seeking a country, and desiring a better country, that is, a Heavenly, for God hath prepared for them a City (Heb. 11. 16).

Just as there are thrones, dominions, principalities and powers among the angelic hosts, so will there be different ranks of redeemed saints, the Antediluvian saints, the Postdiluvian saints, the Church, the Tribulation saints, etc., and differing glories in each as one star differeth from another star in glory (1 Cor. 15. 41). Transcendent beyond all, by grace alone, will all the ransomed Church of God, "from Him, for Him made," be one in and with Christ (John 17. 21, 22) sharing His acquired glory, and beholding His intrinsic eternal glory; no doubt, symbolised by the crowned and throned four and twenty elders, sitting round about the Throne (Rev. 5. 4).

II. **WHERE, AND HOW FAR, IS HEAVEN**?

Again many Scriptures from both Testaments give the situation of Heaven as *"above."*

The children of Israel at the giving of the Law of Moses were forbidden to make any likeness of anything that is in Heaven *above* (Exod. 20. 4). Rahab of Jericho confesses her belief: "The Lord your God, He is God in Heaven *above* and in earth beneath" (Josh. 2. 11). Similarly the Lord Jesus says, "I am from *above*" (John 8. 33). Paul speaks of the Jerusalem which is *above* (Gal. 4. 26).

A little more precision as to the location of Heaven is given us in that remarkable passage in the prophecy of Isaiah (ch. 14. 12-20), which deals with the fall of Lucifer, who is represented as saying (v. 13): "I will ascend into Heaven, I will exalt my throne above the stars of God; I will sit also upon the mount of the congregation in the sides *of the north.*"

As to the interesting problem: How far is Heaven above, the abode of God over all, blessed for ever, it is impossible to estimate it in terms of distance. A Scripture bearing on the problem seems to be found in Daniel 9, where the prophet set his face to seek the Lord his God (vv. 3, 4). Now, while he was speaking the angel Gabriel, being caused to fly swiftly, touched him and informed him at the beginning of his supplications, the commandment came forth and he was sent to show him, etc. (vv. 20-23), and then follows the celebrated prophecy of the seventy weeks. Now Daniel's prayer can be read through at a proper reading rate in about two and a half minutes, or 150 seconds. Hence an angel flying swiftly can come from Heaven to earth in that space of time.

Now, suppose the sun were Heaven, scientists estimate its distance from the earth to be roughly 93,000,000 miles, and the speed of light to be 186,000 miles per second. Hence a little simple division shows that the ray of light takes 500 seconds to reach the earth. But Gabriel accomplished the distance—remember our assumption of the sun being Heaven—in 150 seconds, hence he would have travelled at three and one-third times the speed of light, namely, 620,000 *miles per second*, a speed which staggers the human imagination! *But the sun is not Heaven*, it is far below it, for the light of the nearest fixed star takes seven *years* to reach the earth! Hence the distance of Heaven is entirely beyond human computation, and it appears as if time and space have barely existence in the realm of spirits. Does not Paul speak of "absent from the body, present with the Lord" (2 Cor. 5. 8), as if not a second's time separated the two spheres of the believer's existence?

III. WHAT ARE THE BLESSINGS OF HEAVEN?

Numbers of great and wondrous blessings are recorded in the pages of God's Word, but it would seem that God will delight in continually unfolding and bestowing fresh blessings upon the redeemed throughout all eternity, in the light of Eph. 2. 7, "that in the Ages to Come He might show the exceeding riches of His grace in His kindness towards us through Jesus Christ. " But we feel that every loyal and true-hearted believer in Christ will put at the head of the list:

1. Being with the Lord Jesus and Made Like unto Him.

"Where Jesus is, 'tis Heaven, " and to be out of His presence would be no Heaven at all to the redeemed saint of God. But He has gone to prepare a Place in the many mansions for us, and He is Coming again to receive us unto Himself, that where He is, there we may be also (John 14. 1-3). God in His gracious calling has pre-destinated the believer to be conformed to the image of His Son (Rom. 8. 29), and we shall be made like Him *bodily*, "for He shall change our body of humiliation that it may be fashioned like to the body of His glory" (Phil. 3. 21., R.V.), and *morally*, for "we shall be like Him, for we shall see Him as He is" (1 John 3. 2). The believer will every way be made capable of enjoying the company and presence of His blessed and glorified Lord, and His surroundings in eternity.

2. In Sharing His acquired Glory, and seeing His personal Inherent Glory.

Peter speaks of the sufferings of Christ and the glories that should follow (1 Peter 1. 11, R.V.). There are glories the Lord Jesus acquired as the result of His perfect obedience

unto death on the Cross; these, through grace
alone, He bestows on His people (John 17.
22). But His inherent glory as Son of God,
the glory which He had with the Father before
the world was, can never be bestowed on saved
sinners, but we shall be with Him where He is
that we may behold it (John 17. 24). Blessed
be God, when Christ who is our life, shall be
manifested, we also shall be manifested with
Him—and in glory (Col. 3. 4). Many other
Scriptures bearing on this section of our subject,
and indeed of all its sections, will readily
occur to the minds of our readers.

3. **Eternal Life and Eternal Inheritance there will be the believers' Portion.**

For he is called unto an inheritance incorruptible, for it cannot be ruined or lost by
death; undefiled, for it cannot be marred by
sin; that fadeth not away—as all earthly
things do sooner or later; for it is reserved in
Heaven for him who is kept by the power of
God unto salvation, ready to be revealed in
the last time (1 Peter 1. 4. 5. See also Acts
26. 18; Col. 1. 12; Rev. 1. 7).

4. **Freedom from Sin.**

Sin will be a thing of the past in Heaven;
yet the memory of redemption from it, eternally
the source of praise (Rev. 1. 5; 5. 9, etc.).
And hence there will be in Heaven what there
cannot be now on earth, viz.,

5. We Shall have Reached Perfection.

Spiritually (Rom. 8. 29; Rev. 22. 4); bodily (1 John 3. 2; Phil. 3. 21; 1 Cor. 15. 42-44), and intellectually (1 Cor. 13. 12).   Grand it is to contemplate that we, who know nothing yet as we ought to know, shall then know even as we are known, and shall then be so constituted that perfect knowledge will be accompanied by perfect humility, in contrast with this present earthly state, where out little knowledge tends to puff us up.   And undoubtedly with perfect knowledge there will be perfect worship, perfect love, perfect holiness, and perfect service (Rev. 4. 5; 22. 3; 1 John 4. 17; Eph. 5. 27).

6. Freedom from All that Mars Earthly Life.

There shall be no more tears, no more death, no more sorrow, no more crying, no more pain, no more curse, no more night, no more sea (Rev. 21. 22).   When God wishes to give us poor mortals with all our earthly troubles, some idea of Heaven, He does so by telling us of a condition of things where all is removed that spoiled and blighted our life in this "valley of the shadow of death."

7. There will be Reunion with, and Recognition of Our Loved Ones of Earth.

Aye, and not of them only, but of all God's own.   The possession of perfect knowledge, too, would seem to indicate this.   For Peter knew Moses and Elias "in the holy mount," though they had left this scene centuries before. Paul reminds bereaved saints of Thessalonica that sleeping saints would be raised, living ones changed, and both caught up together to be for ever with the Lord (1 Thess. 4). Wherefore, comfort one another (v. 18). Surely the essence of the comfort of reunion would be recognition of one another. Sower and reaper in the Lord's service shall rejoice together (John 4. 36), and Paul describes his converts in Thessalonica as his hope, his joy, his crown in the presence of the Lord Jesus at His Coming (1 Thess. 2. 19, 20; See also Phil. 2. 15, 16; 2 Cor. 1. 14). Mutual recognition, evidently.

In closing, may one remind readers that in that Home above, of life, light, love, peace, joy, and glory beyond all human thought, shall enter the redeemed (Rev. 1. 5, 6; 5. 9; 14. 4), the undefiled (Rev. 21. 27), and the enrolled (Luke 10. 20; Phil. 4. 1; Heb. 12. 23); but not the unrighteous (1 Cor. 6. 9, 10), the fearful, and, above all, the unbelieving (Rev. 21. 17; 22. 15). And does one ask, "What must I do to be in Heaven and share these things?" God's Word replies; "Believe in Christ" (John 3. 16, 17, 36; 5. 24; Acts 16. 31, etc.). "Come," "Take," (Rev. 21. 6; 22. 17).

CHAPTER VII

Glimpses of the Glory Land

By Captain REGINALD WALLIS, Southport

HEAVEN! Who of the sons of men can conceive its blessedness? Heaven is GLORY. That can be articulated, but it cannot be interpreted. Heaven must be *experienced* in the school of heart education. It cannot be explored or explained. Theological exegesis disappoints the heart. Only as the believer lives experimentally with the Risen Lord in the "Heavenly Places" can he be instructed in the reality of Heaven. Even then, the saintliest child of God will surely be lost in wonder, love and praise before the dazzling glory, the effulgent brightness and the radiant beauty of the Heavenly Jerusalem. "Not half of that City's bright glory, to mortals has ever been told."

A dear old negro saint was once asked what he would do if, on arrival at the place he thought was Heaven, he was informed that the Gospel story was a myth, Heaven was not a reality, and that he had been deceived. "Well" said the old warrior, "I'll just say dat I had a *good time getting here, anyway.*"

1. What does the Holy Spirit Mean by Heaven?

Divine revelation as to the Gloryland is limited (1 John 3. 2). DR. CHALMERS wisely urges, however, that "while we attempt not to be wise *above* that which is written, we should attempt, and that most studiously, to be wise *up to that which* is written."

PAUL and JOHN, of course, could give us first-hand information on the subject. If beloved Paul were asked with what authority he spoke of the future Home of the ransomed, he might say, "Ah, I have had a glimpse of it for myself. My first vision was on the Damascus road. I was blinded by a Heavenly radiance above the brightness of the sun. Then again, I was actually *in Heaven* for a never to be forgotten experience (2 Cor. 12. 2-4). Its glory beggars all description. It is 'unutterable.' I can only say it is 'very far better' than the loftiest experience of Heavenly glory here below."

And the Apostle whom Jesus loved might well add, "Yes, and for me too a door was opened in Heaven, and I saw the Lord *Himself*. That was all. HE was Heaven. I fell at His feet as one dead!" Yes, that is it; whether here in spirit, or there in actuality, a vision of the Lord Jesus is the only unveiling of Heaven. "Where Jesus is, 'tis Heaven there."

The Fulness of HEAVEN is JESUS HIMSELF.

The duration of HEAVEN is the ETERNITY OF JESUS.

The Light of HEAVEN IS THE FACE OF JESUS.

The Joy of HEAVEN IS the PRESENCE OF JESUS.

The Melody of HEAVEN is the NAME OF JESUS.

The Harmony of HEAVEN is the PRAISE OF JESUS.

The Theme of HEAVEN is the WORK OF JESUS.

The Employment of HEAVEN is the SERVICE OF JESUS.

Note, firstly, then, that

I. The Word Teaches that Heaven is:

1. **A Kingdom** (Matt. 18. 23). It is a region where the unrivalled supremacy of the King of kings is acknowledged. It is, therefore perfect in its constitution, just and merciful in its laws, and immaculate in its administration. Praise God. What a contrast to the corruption of earthly politics!

2. **An Abiding City** (Heb. 13. 14; Rev. 21. 21). It is unshakeable in its foundations, and never hoary with the years. It is glorious in its architecture, and its construction (Heb. 11. 10). It is the City of the Living God (Heb. 12. 22). It glories in having "Jesus for its King, angels for its guards, and saints for its citizens." Its walls are Salvation and its gates Praise.

3. **A Reserved Inheritance** (Col. 1. 12). As such it is retained inviolate for *all* who are

"meet to be partakers." Unlike an earthly
heritage, it can never be forfeited or withdrawn.

4. **The Believers' Home** (John 14. 2).
What tender, beautiful memories cluster round
the word *"home."* It cannot be described in
terms of material things. The words "house"
and "mansion" leave the heart cold, but the
mention of *home* quickens the pulse and warms
the spirit. Heaven is a glorious climax, a
goal of desire, the consummate joy and rest
of the pilgrims.

5. **A Sabbath Rest** (Heb. 4. 9, R.V.). It
will not be the rest of passivity or idleness, as
we shall see later. Conflict with the flesh and
the Devil will be over for ever, and all antago-
nistic elements will be eliminated. This is
the heritage of the "People of God."

6. **A Land of Pure Delight** (Rev. 7. 16,
17). The happy voices of children will be
heard in its streets, for "of such is the Kingdom of Heaven." Supreme happiness will
reign there. The Heavenly courts will resound
with Divine melody, and no croaking voices
or jarring discords shall ever mar the eternal
harmony. The saints shall not rest day or
night in their glad ascription of worship to
the enthroned and victorious Lamb. They shall
be crowned with everlasting joy and gladness.

"When we've been there ten thousand years, bright
shining as the sun,
We'll have no less time to sing His praise than when
we first begun."

HALLELUJAH!

Oh, beloved children of God, let us get our hearts into tune here and now. Let not the harp be hung upon the drooping willow tree. Let not the Adversary apply the soft pedal, or silence the "Hallelujahs." Let us often sing of the glories of Heaven on the way there.

There shall be no more sorrow or sighing, clouds of shadows. Gloom will give place to glory, and the sigh to a song. There will be no more mourning over wayward loved ones, and no hearts that bleed with crushing grief and anguish. There will be no tears there; no sickness and no pain; no heart-breaking farewells at the sick-beds of loved ones; no heavy-footed trudge to the mournful graveside. The last great enemy, DEATH, will be for ever vanquished. No sin shall mar the splendour of that beautiful land. No unclean or abominable thing shall ever enter in, or anything false or deceptive. There will be no dens of iniquity, no saloons, no filth and no shame. All the dread effects of the Fall shall be for ever banished. Consider, secondly:

II. What Kind of People will be There?

1. **The Redeemed shall walk there**. Not respectable religionists, but deep-dyed sinners who have been redeemed by the precious blood of Christ. An old Negro Spiritual says, "Everybody talkin' 'bout Heaven ain't goin' dar." True! John Newton exclaims, "If ever I reach Heaven I expect to find three wonders there. First, to meet some one I had never

thought to see there; second, to meet someone whom I had expected to miss there; but third, the greatest wonder of all will be to find myself there."

2. All the inhabitants of Heaven will enjoy **tri-partite perfection**. (1) PHYSICALLY (1 John 3. 1-2). On earth the believer is a redeemed spirit living in an untransformed body. Then, he shall be clothed upon with a radiant resurrection body. No dread diseases, or lingering sicknesses will hamper the body or herald the icy Hand of Death. The saints shall be "Glorified together with Him." (2) MENTALLY. There will be no mental deficiency in Heaven. Here on earth the human mind, even the sanest and wisest, has become aberrant, in greater or lesser degree, because of sin. Then shall the perfect mind of Christ be fully realised in His loved ones. (3) SPIRITUALLY. The Church will rejoice in an unblemished glory (Eph. 5. 27). The glorious Head shall find in her no cause for reproof (1 Cor. 1. 8). His Body shall not only be blameless, but faultless (Jude 24). A perfect Love will be manifested by all (1 John 4. 18), and there will be unquestioned obedience and loyalty (Rev. 7. 15). Let us next consider:

III. What will be the Superlative Blessings of Heaven?

I suggest two: Firstly, and paramountly, **the unspeakable joy of seeing and being with Christ** (1 Cor. 13. 12; Phil. 1. 23). To actually see the King in His beauty, face to face, will eclipse all other Heavenly glory, however magnificent. Faith shall be turned into sight, and one unveiled look into His wonderful face will reveal the full "knowledge of the glory of God." This will be all the Heaven we want, and certainly all we need.

LUTHER said he would rather be in Hell with God's presence, than in Heaven without it.

Secondly, **the Re-Union of Loved Ones**. Shall we recognise our loved ones in Heaven? Shall I know my devoted mother to whose prayers I owe everything? It cannot conceivably be otherwise. Old Testament saints are spoken of, in death, as going to "their own people." Luke 13. 28 also implies clearly the recognition of loved ones in the Better Land. The deeply-implanted longing in the human heart to be with, and to love, dear ones is surely God-given, and will not be disappointed up there. Further:

IV. How shall the Saints be Employed in Heaven?

They will be busily active, though it will not be the little boy's conception of "sitting on clouds and playing harps." It will be a scene of unhindered activity and glorious service. Nor is this incompatible with the idea of true *rest*. Rest is not idleness. Inertia is of the earth, earthy. It tends to weariness. In Heaven, great minds of earth will continue their deep meditations, freed from human

5

limitations and distractions.   Indefatigable
workers will pursue their ceaseless engage-
ments, yet with feet unclogged by the cum-
bersome clay of earth.   What happy conversa-
tions there will be, also, as the saints rehearse
the great things the Lord has done for and with
them.

There will be no carnal gossip in Heaven.
Every conversation will be Christ-exalting.
Would God that we might now seek to follow
the pattern of the Heavens!   All ecclesiastical
and doctrinal wranglings will cease.   There will
be no more controversy about Election and
Freewill, Pre- or Post-Tribulation theories,
and the 1001 other points of dispute which the
Devil uses to separate the people of God to-day.
There will be no denominational arguments,
either!   It will be a holy convocation of the
Redeemed throng who come from the east and
the west, the north and the south, to sit down
in the Kingdom.   What a fellowship!   And
as we look back over the vicissitudes of the
earthly pilgrimage, how we'll bless the Hand
that guided and the Heart that planned!
Lastly:

V. **What is the Practical Relation between Present Grace and Future Glory**?

It should ever be remembered that as the
Lord Jesus is preparing Heaven for the saints
(Matt. 25. 34; John 14. 1-2), so the Holy
Spirit is now *preparing the saints for Heaven*.
Of course, it is recognised that all who have

been justified will certainly be glorified (Rom.
8. 30). "Our title to glory we read in His
Blood. " In these days of coldness and departure, however, a further truth needs to be
emphasised. There will doubtless be **degrees
of Glory in Heaven** among the saints, *de-
pending entirely upon the cultivation of Christ-
likeness on earth and the measure of Grace here
below* (1 Cor. 15. 41-2). Whilst all believers
will be *Constitutionally* like Christ, and perfectly happy according to their capacity, yet
these *capacities* will vary there as they do here.
"Degrees of glory hereafter in Heaven will
depend upon degrees of Grace here on earth. "
This is a vitally important *subjective* verity.
Whilst salvation is truly all of Grace, let us
not presume upon such Grace, or entertain a
carnal conception of the sovereignty of God.
In a very real sense every believer is the maker
of his own destiny, not only as to his eternal
destiny through justifying faith, but as to the
grade of Glory he will possess in the Heavenly
realm. The manifested glory of that blessed
time will be the outer radiance of the inner
life of Christ (Col. 3. 4). Here upon earth,
the urge of the Holy Spirit among the saints
is for a *progressive translation* into His image,
from glory to glory, unto the perfect Day
(2 Cor. 3. 18; Dan. 12. 3). Positions of future
Kingdom authority and degrees of glory are
determined here on earth (Matt. 25. 20-23;
Luke 19. 12-13).

This is verily an arresting and yet inspiring

thought.   May the very Spirit of Heaven be infused into our hearts these days, that the dear Lord may find in His people that upon which He has set His heart.   Earthly faithfulness is never detached from Heavenly reward in glory, and He is "not unmindful to forget . . . "   We shall be *there* in spirit, what we are here.

Whose, then, is the Kingdom of HEAVEN? It belongs to the "pure in heart," and to those who suffer for righteousness' sake (Matt. 5. 10). The Heavenly treasure is being laid up *now* (Matt. 6. 20; 19. 21), and vessels of mercy must be *"prepared* unto glory." To share His eternal glory in Heaven, there must ever be the willingness to take the same pathway as He took.   That is the way of the Cross.   "Let this mind be in you . . . "

CHAPTER VIII

Seven Remarkable Things about Heaven

By JOHN BLOORE, New Jersey

I. The Terms Used for Heaven.

"HEAVEN" is applied to the atmosphere in which the birds fly, and so we read repeatedly of "the fowls of Heaven." Again, it is used of the expanse in which the stars are placed, and they are called the "stars of Heaven." Then, too, God is spoken of as "the God of Heaven." From there He looks down (Deut. 26. 15; Isa. 63. 15; Psa. 33. 13, 14; 80. 14). The term applies to His dwelling place—the third Heaven

II. The Inhabitants of Heaven.

The last use of the term just mentioned brings Heaven before us as a sphere of habitation. One of old "saw the Lord sitting on the throne, and the host of Heaven standing by Him" (1 Kings. 22. 19; 2 Chron. 18. 18). From that sphere angels have descended in time past, they are called "the angels of Heaven" (Matt. 24. 36). He who is "the Second Man, is the Lord from (out of) Heaven" (1 Cor. 15. 47; John 6. 38); from there He will descend, and be revealed (1 Thess. 1. 10; 4. 16; 2 Thess. 1. 7). From thence the Holy Spirit descended, and He came from the Father who is in Heaven (John 14. 16, 17; Acts 2; Matt. 5. 16, 43).

So Heaven is the dwelling place of these Divine Persons, and of those created hosts of spirit beings which surround them. It is the place into which the Lord was received at His ascension (Luke 24. 51; Acts 1. 11; 3. 21; Heb. 9. 24; 1 Peter 3. 22). There Stephen saw Him, and there He appears before God for us. To that sphere, called "the third Heaven" and "Paradise," Paul was caught up and heard unspeakable words.

Heaven is where the believer's hope is laid up (Col. 1. 5), there his "better substance" is found (Heb. 10. 24,) there his inheritance, which is incorruptible, undefiled, and never fades away, is reserved (1 Peter 1. 4). It is therefore, the place to which our Coming Saviour will take us, for our commonwealth is in Heaven (Phil. 3. 20, 21, J.N.D.), and it is the Father's House with many abiding places where we shall be with the Lord for ever. To inhabit that place we must be changed, being made as to our bodies like the Heavenly One (1 Cor. 15).

From these Scriptures we gather that the inhabitants of Heaven are and will be GOD THE FATHER; GOD, THE SON; GOD, THE HOLY SPIRIT; MYRIADS OF HOLY ANGELS; THE RE DEEMED OF PAST AND FUTURE AGES OF TIME, except those of Israel and the nations who will dwell upon the Millennial earth and afterwards inhabit the new earth of the eternal state.

III. **The Location of Heaven**.

The Lord Jesus set this glorious sphere of habitation before His disciples as their Home with Him. He was going there first, and He spoke of the way being known to them. Seemingly thinking in terms of locality, of geography, Thomas said: "Lord, we know not whither Thou goest; and how can we know the way?" Surely if the Lord had wished to give information as to location, that would seem to be the opportune moment; especially, too, since it was on the eve of His return to the Father. His answer leaves us without material or physical indication, but simply directs the searching eye, the longing heart, the pilgrim's hope to HIMSELF. There is nothing given to gratify curiosity as to distance or location to that House where the Father dwells.

Again, Paul is transported to that blessed sphere, but neither is he permitted to give information as to locality. It is as a man in Christ that he is taken up there, and from Adam's race it is only those who are such that will ever enter there. Neither can they enter there in the image of the earthly, it must be as in the image of the Heavenly One—as being conformed to the image of God's Son. *He is everything and all as to the way thither, the*

*truth concerning it, and the Life pervading it
and filling the redeemed who shall dwell there.* Is
not this sufficient for hearts won by His love
—the love He proved in the unequalled sorrow
of the Cross, where He gave Himself for us?

IV. **The Description of Heaven.**

If location is not fixed, we are not left, however, without that which is descriptive of what
Heaven really means. Certain statements are
made, and terms used which serve to convey to
us according to our present capacity a conception of this blessed and glorious place.

1. "MY FATHER'S HOUSE" (John 14. 2).
That brings before us all the precious intimacies of home, its love, kindredness of spirit,
mutual interests, service, rest, joy, pleasures,
all in the known relationship of children.
Now already our Christian homes where the
Father, Son, and Holy Spirit are known,
where the truth is dwelling through grace,
should be just a little picture of that blessed
and happy home-dwelling with our Father
who is in Heaven.

2. "PARADISE" (2 Cor. 12. 4), the apostle
calls it, by which in a word he presents the
idea of its inexpressible beauty, as it is also
the place where words are uttered unspeakable
by lips of flesh and blood. In its midst, "the
midst of the Paradise of God" (Rev. 2. 7),
is the Tree of Life of which the overcomer will
eat.

3. "AN HEAVENLY COUNTRY" (Heb. 11.

16). Of it we are citizens, it is our common-wealth, and what we know "country" means to us now as creatures of earth will be known in perfection, without one thing to mar or disturb, in that Heaven into which we shall be ushered at the Coming of the Lord.

4. "THE CITY TO COME" (Heb. 11. 16)—the city God "hath prepared" for those who are "strangers and pilgrims on the earth." This city is firmly founded, its builder and maker is God. Man's cities do not continue, they rise on a cursed earth and crumble into dust, like their makers they fall into decay and perish. "Here *we* have no continuing city, we seek one to come" (Heb. 13. 14). From the use of this figure we gather still another idea of our "eternal inheritance," which is "reserved in Heaven." And then we have it named. It is

5. "THE HEAVENLY JERUSALEM" (Heb. 12. 22)—that holy city which comes down from God out of Heaven as a Bride adorned for her husband. This is "the city of My God," as the Lord speaks to the overcomer in Rev. 3. 12. How beautifully suggestive the name—Jerusalem, "the foundation of peace." Upon that foundation God builds that blessed and glorious system of things which will constitute our eternal sphere of habitation. It is peace made by the Blood of the Cross, on this basis reconciliation is effected in perfect agreement with the fulness of the Godhead (Col. 1. 19). That foundation shall never be shaken,

never moved, the peace of that city never broken, its order never disturbed, it abides for ever in its beauty, freshness, holiness, and glory, God's eternal tabernacle among men.

Consider the description of this city in Rev. 21:—

It is Divine in its character—*"holy."*

It is heavenly, not earthly—*"out of heaven."*

It is Divine in origin—*"from God."*

It is Divine in glory—*"having the glory of God."*

It has perfect security—*"a wall great and high."*

It has the perfection of governmental administrative power—*"twelve gates,"* etc.

Its foundations take their character from names in them—*"the twelve apostles of the Lamb."*

It is foursquare—*perfect equality, equity, righteousness.*

It is the Divine centre.

It is full of Divine light.

It is absolutely pure.

V. The Bliss of Heaven.

What a glorious scene of perpetual blessedness is the city of our God! Its bliss is assured for all that has brought the opposite is for ever excluded. Every force of evil is in its own place, *"without,"* and can never rise again to disturb or mar God's new creation.

Its supreme happiness will be found in that full and unhindered fellowship which will be enjoyed with the Father and the Son in the power of the Holy Spirit. Then shall God be all in all to all His creatures, and in all His creation. In that which we now know and enjoy we have "the firstfruits of the Spirit." How blessed will be the full harvest in Glory!

VI. The Permanence of Heaven.

We receive "a Kingdom which cannot be moved" (Heb. 12. 28). Our entrance is "into the everlasting kingdom of our Lord and Saviour, Jesus Christ" (2 Pet. 1. 11). Christ is the appointed Heir of all things, and we are His joint-heirs. He will subjugate all things in Heaven and on earth, and then deliver up the Kingdom to the Father, that GOD— FATHER, SON and HOLY SPIRIT—may be all in all. The Gospel is the Gospel of the "everlasting (eternal) God" (Rom. 16. 25, 26), and ours is "eternal inheritance" (Heb. 9. 15), and the life in which we enjoy it is "eternal life." Our salvation is "in Christ Jesus with eternal glory" (2 Tim. 2. 10), and God has called us to "His eternal glory" (1 Peter 5. 10; 1 Thess. 2. 12).

VII. The Glory of Heaven.

The Lord assures us that where He is there we shall be also. The glory that we shall behold there is His glory (John 17. 24). Scriptures already referred to indicate that it is

God's glory which fills all that place.   The
Lamb is the lamp of it (Rev. 21. 23, J.N.D.).

*   *   *   *   *   *

"Wherefore, beloved, seeing that ye look
for such things, be diligent that ye may be
found of Him in peace, without spot, and
blameless" (2 Peter 3. 14).

"Grow in grace, and in the knowledge of our
Lord and Saviour, Jesus Christ.   To Him be
glory both now and for ever.   Amen" (2 Peter
3. 18).

CHAPTER IX

Some Misrepresentations about Heaven

By HAROLD P. BARKER, Paignton

THERE are a few elementary data to which we must give heed by way of preparation for a study of this tremendous subject.

We find

Three Heavens Mentioned in Scripture.

First, the ATMOSPHERIC HEAVENS that surround the earth. Here our little feathered friends fly, "birds of the heavens," as they are called (Jer. 4. 25).

Second, the STELLAR HEAVENS, to which we look up with awe and amazement by night. Here shine those glorious orbs that testify to the creative wisdom and power of God. So we read of "the stars of heaven and the constellations thereof" (Isaiah 13. 10).

Third, the Heaven to which Christ is gone, the HEAVEN OF OUR HOPES and longings. It is called "the third Heaven" in 2 Cor. 12. 2.

Are all these Heavens *places*? One can hardly speak of the air surrounding the globe as a "place." And the starry Heavens? Why, as far as human knowledge goes, they are commensurate with illimitable space!

Still less can we think of the **Heaven of Heavens in Terms of Geography or Locality**. When our Lord "looked up to heaven" in Mark 6. 41, it was during the day; evening had not yet come (verse 47). But when on the night of His betrayal He offered His wonderful prayer recorded in John 17, He still "lifted up His eyes to Heaven." But He looked in an entirely different direction! What is above our heads at noon is beneath our feet at midnight.

When we pray we look up to Heaven. Our brethren in Australia do the same. But they, if praying at the same time, look in a diametrically different direction. Yet, both they and we, are looking up to Heaven.

If Heaven were a fixed locality; if, for instance, it were behind any particular group of stars, we could only look up to Heaven when the earth is in a certain position, and those stars in the firmament above our heads.

But to the Heaven of the Bible we may *always* look up. In our thoughts it is above us; it is the home of our souls, whether in Europe or Australia. Is not this sufficient to show that Heaven is not the name of a limited locality? If it were, we could not at all times and in all places, look up to it. We do not, therefore, regard the word "Heaven" as a *topographical* term (see note at end of this chapter).

Again, we must not make the crude and elementary mistake of confounding Heaven with "that great city, **the Holy Jerusalem**" of Rev. 21. 10, which John in vision, saw descending out *of heaven*. Surely it is clear to any one of ordinary intelligence that what comes out of Heaven cannot BE Heaven!

The angel said to John (in vision): "I will show thee the bride, the Lamb's wife," and immediately proceeded to show him the holy Jerusalem. It is the Bride, set forth under the figure of a city. What this suggests is that *the administration* of "the world to come" (the Millennium) will not be, as in ages past, by means of angels (Heb. 2. 5), but through the saints of the present dispensation, who compose the Bride. The nations of the saved are to walk in the light of the city (Rev. 21. 24). That is, I take it, that Heavenly influences will be brought to bear upon men on earth for their guidance by those who have learned God in the present period of grace.

In the first four verses of Rev. 21, the holy city is seen in

Her Eternal Glory,

the tabernacle by means of which God dwells with men when the new Heaven and the New Earth have come into being. There will be no "nations" and "kings" then.

But from verse 10 onward the vision goes back and presents the city (*i.e.*, the Bride) filling her place in "the world to come," then there will still be nations and kings (verse 24). In chap. 22, the vision enlarges somewhat and

shows us more the surroundings, the home, the
eternal state of the Bride.   If any one says,
"Well, this at all events is Heaven!" I shall
heartily agree.   Only, it is the Heaven of the
future, not the Heaven of to-day.

There are, of course, many differences
between the city (the Bride) and Heaven.
To mention one more will suffice.   There was

no temple seen in the city

(Rev. 21. 22) ; but in Heaven John saw a temple
(Rev. 11. 19).

The city of Rev. 21 having come down out
of Heaven, we cannot make deductions as to
what Heaven is like from the study of it ; our
concern is rather as to *what was left behind*
when the city was seen descending out of
Heaven.

Now for our little talk on Heaven itself.   It
must necessarily be meagre, for our data are few.

It is sometimes said that

the Presence of Jesus will make Heaven

for us.   True indeed!   What would Heaven
be without Him for those who love Him?

I do not forget for a moment that all Divine
attributes were His, omnipresence among them.
But as a Man He was only in one place at a
time.   Of Bethany He said: "I was not there"
(John 11. 15).   Of the empty grave the angel
said: "He is not here" (Mark 16. 6).   So there
were places on earth where He was not, and
we are, therefore, justified in saying that in

the same way He was not in Heaven. As a Man
here He looked up to Heaven. He was not
there in *bodily presence*.

Some may refer to John 1. 18, "No man hath
seen God at any time; the only begotten Son,
which is in the Bosom of the Father, He hath
revealed Him."

The Bosom of the Father

surely means the Father's affections, where
the Son ever dwelt, whether in Heaven from
all eternity or as a Man here on earth.

We may here quote *as a suggestion* what the
late W. H. Dorman used to speak of Rev. 4.:
"After this I looked, and, behold, a door was
opened in Heaven; and the first voice which I
heard was as it were of a trumpet talking
with me, which said, Come up hither. . . ."

He called it a picture of

"A Christless Heaven."

He believed that it carries us there in thought
during the time that Christ was on earth. He
is clearly not in Heaven when the question of
Rev. 5. 2 is asked. For *"no man in Heaven*
was found worthy to open the book." But
neither was there one on earth. Where, then,
was the Lord Jesus? Mr. Dorman answered
the question by a reference to John 12. 32.
It was at the moment that Christ was on the
Cross, "lifted up from the earth." Immediately
afterwards the announcement is made in Heaven
of a great victory: "The Lion of the tribe of
Judah . . . hath prevailed." John gazes, and

6

sees suddenly appear in Heaven "a lamb as it had been slain." It was

The Victor of Calvary,

returned to Heaven from the arena of His triumph on earth. Then, for the first time, the great redemption song is raised, and all Heaven joins in acclaiming the Lamb as worthy.

The Heavens have always been profoundly interested in God's ways with men on earth. They have listened to His lament over the backsliding of the beloved nation (Isa. 1. 2); they have been "astonished" and "desolate" at the sight of man's sin and ingratitude. (Jer. 2. 12), and full of joy, many a time over the repentance of even one sinner (Luke 15. 7).

As to

Our Future in Heaven,

two things are certain. First, that *we shall never be infinite*, never Divine, never possessed of the attributes of Deity. Second, that we shall always be *in the presence of the Infinite*.

Therefore, there will eternally be something beyond us and above us. For we can never compass infinity. There will for ever be something fresh to learn about God, fresh unveilings of Himself, even as there have been during the course of the ages on earth.

Perhaps this is why the word "eternity" is not used in describing our life in Heaven, but "the ages to come" (Eph. 2. 7). Each age will be marked by a fresh revelation of God, and that revelation will characterise the age, even as various revelations of Himself have characterised the successive ages of time.

So that in the Heavens

We Shall Find No Monotony.

There will always be fresh cause for wonder and worship. But in all the ages the result will be glory to God by Christ Jesus, the Assembly being the vessel thereof (Eph. 3. 21).

Probably when the present heavens and earth have perished (Heb. 1. 11), and the new Heavens and new earth have been formed (2 Peter 3. 13), there will not be much difference between them. For God, by means of His Tabernacle (compare Eph. 2. 22) will dwell with men. They will be His happy flock and eternally He will find His pleasure in them.

This is what Heaven in the future, after the years of Millennial glory have rolled by, will mean for God and for us.

Note.—Some have seen a reference to Heaven in Job 26. 7. But this is fanciful. Read the verse as in the New Translation (M.): "The northern skies He spreads o'er empty space, and hangs the earth on nothing." The patriarch is expressing his wonder at God's power. Gazing northward, he sees the sky by night studded with thousands of shining orbs, yet supported by no material foundation. These thousands of stars are all suspended over an empty space; the very earth is hung upon nothing. To read into this passage a discovery of a sphere in space that is void of stars is hardly permissible. It was the fact of all the stars with which (from his viewpoint) the northern skies were filled, yet stretched out over nothing, that filled the observer with wonder at the Divine power that could do even this.

CHAPTER X

The Heaven that is to Be

By W. E. VINE, M.A., Bath

SCRIPTURE makes a distinction between the Heaven which forms the subject of our consideration, and the physical heavens. The distinction lies especially in relation to the Person of Christ. The created Heaven consist of two regions, the lower, which surrounds the earth, in which rain, for instance, falls, (Deut. 11. 11), and birds fly (Matt. 6. 26, R.V.), "the birds of the Heaven"), and the higher, where the stars are (Matt. 24. 28). Beyond these is the place where Christ has ascended. He has been "made higher than the Heavens" (Heb. 7. 26). At His ascension He passed "through the Heavens" (Heb. 4. 14, R.V.). through the created regions and beyond them into Heaven itself. He ascended, "far above all the Heavens." Again, "Christ entered not into a holy place made with hands, like in pattern to the true; but into Heaven itself, now to appear before the face of God for us" (Heb. 9. 24, R.V.). Here God ever dwelt, Father, Son, and Holy Spirit, in all the effulgence of self-existent glory. From that glory, which the Son had with the Father before the world was, the Father sent Him.

The Apostle Paul speaks of this region as

"The Third Heaven."

Thither he was caught up, and there he heard "unspeakable words which it is not lawful (*margin*, "possible") for man to utter" (2 Cor. 12. 4).

It was evidently the Divine intention that we should be

Occupied More with God Himself

than with the wonders and glories of Heaven. God is more important than the locality in which He dwells. Meditation about the blissful region must hold a very secondary place to that of communion with the Lord Himself. And, after all, the loveliness of Heaven consists less in its circumstantial grandeur and glory than in the beauty of holiness and moral conformity to Christ. Hence the purposive economy of detail about the locality.

Heaven not Merely a Condition.

The passages quoted above make clear that Heaven is a place. Christ's own words were, "I go to prepare a place for you" (John 14. 3).

Paul speaks of the place where he was caught up as Paradise. The word signifies an enclosure the circumstances of which are those of happiness. It is a place where the Lord promised the penitent malefactor that he would be with Him that very day* (Luke 23. 43).

He also calls it "the Paradise of God" (Rev. 2. 7). While Heaven is a place, the idea of a state or condition is constantly associated with it.

Best of all, Christ Himself makes Heaven what it is. To be absent from the body, at the death of the believer, is to be "at Home with the Lord." "AT HOME!" A sweetly suggestive word! What joyous associations are connected with it! Towards home the mariner on the deep, the soldier in his campaign, the traveller in his wanderings, turn their wistful thoughts. Home, the scene of parental and filial affection, family life and friendships! "At Home with the Lord!" Yes, Christ makes Heaven a home. Paul, to whom Christ was everything here, says that to depart this life is to be with Him, and for that reason is "very far better" (Phil. 1. 23). And when the Lord returns, He says, "I will receive you unto Myself, that where I am, there ye may be also" (John 14. 3).

No Purgatory.

There is nothing between our being absent from the body and being "at Home with the

---

*To attach the word "to-day" to the statement "Verily I say unto thee," is both to rob it of its significance and to remove it from its grammatical position of emphasis in the clause in which it belongs. To think that the Lord should be conceived of as telling the man He was speaking to Him that day! The sweet consolation of His utterances lie in the association of the words "to-day . . . with Me"

Lord. " The idea of purgatory is pure imagination, a deception profitable for those who impose it on their dupes, but without endorsement in the pages of Holy Scripture. Nor is there anything therein to support the notion that believers in their spirit state pass from a lower stage to a higher, or from one degree of blessedness to another. The spirits of the redeemed are the spirits of the just "made perfect" (Heb. 12. 23.) There is doubtless an increase in their knowledge and understanding of God and His ways and His glories as revealed in Christ, and of the exquisite and infinite diversities of omniscient skill; but there is no such things as an increase in fitness for His presence. Those who are here are "in Christ" are "made meet to be partakers of the inheritance of the saints in light" (Col. 1. 12).

That "to be with Christ is very far better" is no doubt what the apostle had in his mind when he said "to die is gain. " The "gain" would be in enjoying more of Christ than had been possible in this life. Moreover, Paul had himself already been in Paradise. What he had seen and heard there intensified His longings to be with his Lord.

No Sleep of the Soul!

How preposterous such testimony makes the doctrine of the sleep of the soul! In the first place, the word "sleep" is never used in Scripture of the spirit; it is said of the *body*. Suggestive of this is the description, "They

that sleep in the dust of the earth" (Dan.
12. 2). The very word "cemetery" signifies
the "sleeping place."

That saints are said to fall asleep is indicative of the cessation of bodily activity.
Not so with the spirit! The spirit enters
into the untrammelled enjoyment of its activities in Paradise. This liberation from the
restrictive conditions of the natural body
Peter describes as the "putting off of my
tabernacle" (2 Peter 1. 14), a vivid description
of the release of the spirit! There is nothing
in Heaven to hinder or disturb the spirit in
its communion with the Lord, and in all the
other activities which are there enjoyed. "In
Thy presence is fulness of joy" (Psa. 16. 11).

"To depart and to be with Christ" could
not be "very far better" if this means to lapse
into unconsciousness, and so to become ob-
livious of one's surroundings. That would be
to enjoy Christ less even than in this life.
It could not be "fulness of joy." To Stephen
it was granted to see "the Heavens open and
the Son of Man standing on the right hand
of God." Stephen's prayer at his martyrdom
was, "Lord Jesus, receive my spirit." Then
with a prayer for the forgiveness of his enemies
"he fell asleep." What folly to conceive of
this as passing into a state of unconsciousness!
No longer even the Heavenly vision! What
an outrageous notion! All around in Paradise
an utter blank! A cessation of the conscious
enjoyment of the Lord and His love till the

resurrection day! What a perversion of the truth! Not in that state did the Lord answer His martyr's prayer and receive his spirit. To press a figure of speech beyond the Divine intention of its application is to prepare the way for erroneous doctrine.

Personal Recognition.

The Scriptures already referred to show that personal recognition is the experience of the departed. This is further confirmed by the Lord's testimony concerning Abraham, Isaac, and Jacob. In reply to the question of the Sadducees, He says, "Have ye not read that which was spoken unto you by God, saying, I am the God of Abraham, and the God of Isaac, and the God of Jacob. God is not the God of the dead, but of the living" (Matt. 22. 32). The conscious relationship between God and the patriarchs in their lifetime has continued ever since. He is still their God. They *live* unto Him" (Luke 20. 38) and ever will.

Recounting the experience of the rich man and Lazarus, the Lord makes clear the matter of recognition in the intermediate state. Lazarus was in the place which the Lord figuratively calls "Abraham's bosom"; it was a place of bliss, separated by an impassable gulf from that region of Hades to which the rich man had gone; His recognition of Abraham continued.

All the theories which have been advanced,

such as that Christ was merely accommodating Himself to the tradition of the Pharisees, or that He was adopting some of the prevalent fictitious conceptions of the time, or exposing the conceits of mere human theology, are outrageous, not to say blasphemous.

Lazarus was evidently in happy intercourse with Abraham. The Douay Version of verse 23, which is based upon the Vulgate, makes out the experience of the rich man to be at the "last day," but the original Greek, faithfully rendered in the A.V. and R.V., makes such an idea impossible. Moreover, it is entirely disproved by the statement, *"Now* he is comforted, and thou art in anguish" (v. 25).

Mutual recognition in the spirit state is confirmed also by John's testimony as to the vision given to him at the opening of the fifth seal. He saw "the souls of them that had been slain for the Word of God and for the testimony which they held; and they cried with a great voice, saying, How long, O Master, the Holy and True, dost Thou not judge and avenge our blood on them that dwell on the earth?" White robes were given to them, and they were told to rest for a little time till the rest of their brethren were killed. Firstly, they are seen to be in the spirit state; secondly, their pleadings are with one consent; thirdly, that which is ministered to them is ministered to their comfort in association one with another. The conclusion as to their mutual recognition is obvious.

We may observe, too, what David says about
his dead child: "Now he is dead, wherefore
should I fast? Can I bring him back again?
I shall go to him, but he shall not return to
me." The idea in his mind was not simply
that he would go to the place where his child
was, nor was it that he would lapse into unconsciousness when he went there; plainly,
his departure to him would involve his recognition of him.

The Happiness of Departed Saints.

What comfort then, the Scriptures give
us as to the present experience of our loved
ones who are at Home with the Lord! How
ineffably blessed is their state! Released from
the body of weariness, sickness, and pain,
freed from this present life with its perplexi-
ties, its uncertainties, its sins and its sighings,
they enjoy a state of rest and peace, of un-
broken fellowship with the Lord and with one
another, and all in an activity unconceivable
to the natural mind, and impossible to the
natural state.

Let it not be imagined that the saints in
Heaven are merely engaged in intercourse.
That is not their sole occupation any more than
it is our single business here. As the angels
who are spirits, are engaged in service for their
Master, so with departed believers. Theirs
is the blessedness, not only of worship and
praise, but of *service* to the Lord. The mode
of this service is not disclosed to us.

No Intermediate Body.

A deduction has been drawn from the opening passage of 2 Cor. 5, that a temporary body is given to the believer upon departing this life. That the statement, "If the earthly house of our tabernacle be dissolved, we have a building from God, a house not made with hands, eternal in the Heavens," refers, not to the intermediate state, but to what takes place at the resurrection, is clear from the context. The apostle speaks of the spirit state as that of being unclothed (verse 4). That we may be clothed upon with our habitation which is from Heaven, is the object of our earnest hope, for then "what is mortal will be swallowed up of life" (verse 4). The phrase "what is mortal" refers to this natural body, and that will be swallowed up of life when the Lord comes to the air to receive us to Himself. Then we shall be supplied with our building from God, the house "not made with hands, eternal in the Heavens."

Heaven, now experienced by the spirits of the just made perfect, will then be enjoyed in full measure in their glorified state. Then, having received their rewards at His judgment-Seat, according to the measure of their adherence to the Word of God and their faithfulness in His service in this life, they will come forth to reign with Him.

That Heaven that is to Be.

What blessedness will be ours in the new Heaven and earth, which are to supersede the

old creation! What glories are depicted in the
symbolism of the City-Bride!—perfection both
of harmoniously regulated organisation, and of
holy intimacy and affection.

That is true already in Heaven which is said
of the eternal state: "Death shall be no more;
neither shall there be mourning, nor crying,
nor pain any more." But the glory of the
Heaven that is to be, is the glory of the City
"which hath the foundations, whose Builder
(Architect) and Maker is God." And the glory
of the city is the glory "of God and of the
Lamb." It will have no need of the sun,
neither of the moon to shine upon it, for
"the glory of God will lighten it and the lamp
therefore is the Lamb." There will be no
temple therein; for "the Lord God the Almighty
and the Lamb, are the temple thereof" (Rev.
21. 22). That there is no temple is indicative
of full and free access to be enjoyed by all the
saints alike. Moreover, as God and the Lamb
will be the Temple, to worship God and Christ
will be to be "in God" and "in Christ," and
to enjoy the full realisation of the Divine
attributes and excellencies.

The association of God and the Lamb indicates that all that is said in connection therewith is established on a basis of redemption.
In this respect there will be perfect recognition
of, and submission to, the sovereign authority
of God: "There shall be no curse any more;
and the throne of God and the Lamb shall be
therein; and His servants shall do Him service"

(22. 3).   Not only will the Father and the Son
be manifested in all their combined glory,
but the service that will be rendered will be
carried out in loving and undeviating sub-
jection to Their rule, the rule of "Our Lord and
His Christ" (11. 15), and in unbounded and
unending gratitude for what infinite wisdom
and love and the wonders of redeeming grace
have wrought.   "They shall see His face, and
His Name shall be in their foreheads." The
vision of His face will involve complete conformity to Him, and the uninterrupted reflection of His character.   His saints will
perfectly represent Him and bear untarnished
testimony to all that He is.

What a contrast to present conditions of
earth!   A city without griefs, without graves,
without sins, without sorrows, a city resplendent with the glory of Him whose highest
handiwork will be the very masterpiece of
God, the means of the reflection of His glory, the
seat and centre of Divine communications!
"'Tis Heaven where Jesus is," and the highest
bliss that we shall enjoy the moment we come
there, and through the ages of eternity, will
be that our eyes shall see "the King in His
beauty," and the vision will mean our transformation into His image.   "We shall be
like Him; for we shall see Him even as He is"
(1 John 3. 2).   Glorious Consummation.

CHAPTER XI

Heaven: The Future Home of the Redeemed

By ANDREW BORLAND, M.A., Irvine

THAT there should be increased interest in the future as recorded in the Bible is a hopeful sign of the times. Whether that is a precursor of a genuine revival among God's people or not, it would be premature to say, but it is to be hoped that the diligence shown in acquiring information with respect to the return of the Lord, will be accompanied as it should be, by a corresponding diligence in being "pure as He is pure" (1 John 3. 3).

I. SOURCES OF INFORMATION.

Man is instinctively inquisitive about the future. Its very uncertainty fascinates him. With irrepressible longing he craves knowledge not only of to-morrow, but also of the life that lies beyond "time's allotted span." In vain does he attempt to extinguish the flame of desire, for in spite of sarcastic protests from his intellectual "superior" fellow-man, the man in the street nurses, at particular occurrences in his life, a prurient inquisitiveness regarding the ultimate end of existence.

Three questions constantly assail the human mind and prompt it to investigation, namely: Whence have I come? Whither am I bound? Why am I here?

Origin, Destiny, Purpose!

Evolution, the supposed panacea for resolving all man's doubts in these concerns! answers the first and second of these questions in terms of a now thread-bare theory that offers no ultimate assurance, and leaves the questioner in a disconcerting quandary regarding the third. If man has come out of "nowhere," and must finally be snuffed out like a candle flame, of what purpose can be his existence in a universe where blind chance rules and man is the plaything of soulless force?

But as the intention of this chapter is strictly limited, it does not fall within its province to discuss matters relating either to the origin or to the purpose of life. Consequently, too, it is not necessary to discuss the question of man's immortality—reason and faith cry out for it, while revelation definitely asserts it. Nor does it fall within the writer's scope to investigate the problem of the destiny of all men; his more pleasant task is to attempt to supply some instruction regarding THE HOME OF THE REDEEMED.

Scientific Investigation.

Enlightment has been sought by questioning souls in various sources. Let us briefly summarise these.

Science, as such, can neither affirm nor deny the possibility of a life of endless bliss in a Heavenly Home prepared by a beneficent Saviour for the children of the Father's House. It may, or it may not, predict a cataclysmic end to the present scheme of the material universe, but it can make no scientific pronouncement regarding the souls of men, each of which, in the estimation of God, is of infinitely more value than are the myriads of stars thrown under view by the magnificent telescopes of our generation. Nowhere in the spatial deeps, raked by the most powerful lenses, have astronomers scanned the Home of the redeemed, and revelled in such beauties as thrilled the heart of the seer, John.

Philosophical Speculation.

Philosophy has for its province the whole universe of knowledge. It builds upon "systems of interpretation," and in vain does the layman, hungering for positive information, sit at the feet of his teacher. It traffics in descriptions of such vague terminology that ordinary individuals are at a loss to discover the meaning of its learned jargon. Heaven for the philosopher is not a definable locality. The word is simply a convenient term for an infinite sphere of existence, so etherialised, so tenuous, that it might as well not be. The soul becomes a wanderer in the vastness of a spiritual world where it finds "God, and its own immortality." Such is the language of philosophy.

7

Spiritualistic Materialisations.

Alert to trade on the natural curiosity of mankind, the Devil, for assuming whose personal existence we need not apologise in this article, has satisfied that craving by communicating through mediums, chosen often for his purpose because of their debased character, information which is a disgusting travesty of the reality, a burlesque of the highest aspirations of the human heart.

With Spiritists, Heaven, the common gathering place of all men, irrespective of their morality or their beliefs, their character or their creed, is a glorified projection of the earth, with its failures as well as its longings. There the inhabitants still have human appetites and human characteristics, eat cakes, drink wine, smoke cigars, and behave themselves just as they please. A *materialised* Heaven is the home of the *Spiritist*!!

That men, eminently sensible and recognised authorities in other walks of life, should be apologists even in the remotest sense, for this recrudescence of an ancient pagan cult is almost past comprehension. Spiritism, in spite of its learned advocates, has nothing to offer of real comfort and joy regarding the abode of the "saints of God."

Uninstructed Imagination.

Even for those of us who do not find our aspirations satisfied in the Heaven of either the scientist, the philosopher, or the Spiritist, how much of our conception of Heaven has been formed by the phraseology of our hymns.

Minds, poetically inclined, have taken the symbolism of an Oriental people and transliterated it into western vocabulary without the slightest explanation of the fact that poetical expressions are not to be taken literally. Some of these hymns present the Home of the redeemed almost as material (if not as grossly so) as the "Heaven" of the Spiritist. Failing to appreciate the meaning of the language of the Scriptures, imagination has been lured into descriptions of bliss that appeal to the senses rather than to the spirit. Quotation is needless, Heaven is pictured as a place where there are "gold-paved streets," encircled by "fields of fadeless green," etc. The symbolism expresses a reality, the sense of which only material concepts could convey to the human understanding. While delighting in the pictorial representation of our future abode, we should constantly remind ourselves that it is still *only representation*.

Divine Revelation.

The only reliable source of information regarding Heaven is the Bible. Such a statement may be trite, but it is none the less true. The veracity of the Bible, proved with regard to the past, may be confidently assumed in its pronouncements regarding the future. From its pages we may derive instruction in our subject in three ways, viz., by direct and specific declaration, by intelligent inference, and by symbolic description.

1. By Direct and Specific Declaration. Scattered throughout the New Testament are affirmations both by the Lord Himself and by His disciples concerning the Home of the redeemed. The Lord spoke with personal authority, the disciples spoke with the authority of personal revelation from the Lord Himself. Such affirmations are couched in terms which admit of no dubiety.

The Declarations are of Certainties,

inviolable because part of the eternal purpose of God.

Philosophising interpreters of the Scriptures rob many passages of their intrinsic worth by spiritualising what is evidently intended to be literal. We shall return to a consideration of these passages later.

2. By Intelligent Inference. By comparing Scripture with Scripture, and by applying legitimate information regarding the "conditions of life" in the eternal state. How prone are we to allow ourselves to forget that one of God's favourite methods of imparting instruction is contained in the words: "Search the Scriptures."

It is recorded of the Bereans that they "searched the Scriptures" (Acts 20. 4), the verb suggesting that they adopted the method that surveyors would when engaged in mapping out a tract of land. That was

Arduous Study of the Word.

We, too, will never arrive at a clear knowledge of the mind of God unless we are prepared to adopt the same method. We may
add to our stock of information from direct
declaration by legitimate inference.

3. By Interpretation of Symbolic Description. Sometimes, but in the main, not
very often, it may be difficult to decide whether
the interpretation should be literal or meta-
phorical, but in most cases the interpretation
of the context will decide for us. If the context is built on symbolism then we may be
almost sure that the separate items are intended to be symbolic. The Book of the
Revelation is the chief source of information
here.

This much, then, may be asserted, that the
Bible is our sole

Source of Reliable Information

regarding the future, and that the conditions
for deriving benefit therefrom are diligent
study and obedient will.

A necessary qualification is the possession
of spiritual affinity with Heavenly things
through the "new birth" (John 3. 3), and the
indwelling of the Holy Spirit, whose work it
is to reveal things to come to those who
patiently seek His guidance. Let us not be wise
above what is written, but let us claim as our
province of investigation the blessed fact

made known regarding the Home to which each saint is travelling and whither for us the Saviour has already gone that He Himself might prepare it for us, awaiting the moment when He will rapture His own to be with Himself. When that takes place, then shall we know in experience what we may learn to anticipate through a knowledge of the Word.

II. **THE FATHER'S HOUSE.**

First personal pronouns are the language of intimacy. As no one else could, Christ spoke of God as "My Father," for He had come, as He Himself stated concerning His mission, to reveal God as the Father. The Jewish nation knew God by revelation as Jehovah, the Creator of the universe, but the Christian Church knows Him as the "God and Father of our Lord Jesus Christ" (Eph. 1. 3). To the Jews the imposing pile of architecture occupying the most prominent position in the city of Jerusalem was known as the Temple of Jehovah. There they worshipped and served Him in the manner prescribed in their Scriptures and through the ritual of the di- vinely-appointed priesthood. The orthodox Jew with spiritual faculty to discern the reality behind the ceremonial observances, trembled as he thought of the august Presence Whose symbol that Temple was.

When, however, Christ came, He disclosed the solitariness of His being, and

The Uniqueness of His Experience,

for He spoke of the Temple in terms of the utmost familiarity, not the familiarity that betokens ignorance and vulgarity, but that indicates knowledge of the most tender intimacy. To Him the building was "My Father's House." It is true that He had no priestly right to function in its symbolical ritual, yet He manifested His superiority to an earthly priesthood by a consciousness that He was at Home in the very place where they performed their services with fear and trembling. With Him was the intimacy of personal acquaintance. His disciples must often have heard Him speak of the Temple as "My Father's House." The term must have worn an impressive meaning to them, since they had learned that He was Christ the Son of the Living God.

Now He is on the eve of departure from them. Towards the revelation He was about to make to them their Master had been bringing them. The time is ripe for further disclosure regarding

His Future and Theirs as Associated

with Him. Taught as they had been in Old Testament literature, and trained in orthodox Jewish thought, these eleven men had belief in a resurrection, but their knowledge of the world beyond the grave was meagre in the extreme. During His sojourn with them, Christ had scattered glimpses about Heaven, but on no occasion had He given them a per-

sonal assurance that His future had a mission
as well as had His present. He had come to
prepare the way to the Father, now, on the
verge of what was to them at least the unseen,
He discloses the fact that His mission as He
went from them was to prepare a place with
the Father for all who would thereafter follow
Him.   How familiar to us have become words
which to these disciples must have been a start-
ling announcement, for they encompass so much
truth that they allow a reverent meditation

Unbounded Scope for Thought

as it traffics in things unseen.

Read His words again, and ponder over
them as you read.   "In MY FATHER'S House
are many mansions: if it were not so, I would
have told you.   I go to prepare a place for you.
And if I go and prepare a place for you, I will
come again and receive you unto Myself; that
where I am, there may ye be also" (John 14. 2, 3).
In such simple, homely language did Christ
make His fullest revelation concerning the
Home of the Redeemed.   The simplicity is
the language of sympathy and sincerity.   The
thoughtful student cannot but notice, and it
is important that he should, that although
the Saviour knew infinitely more about Heaven
than He cared to reveal, He refrained from
making disclosures regarding

The Details of the Home.

And why? Evidently because minds dealing
with a material world in terms of human

language, were as yet incapable of appreciating the "spiritualness" of the realm to which Christ was going and to which He would soon call them. For it is impossible to rid the mind of materialistic concepts in treating of a spiritual world. Our Lord's language, consequently, is vague and guarded, and yet precise enough to convey such information as will enable us to form worthy thoughts regarding that world to which He has gone.

It is noticeable, too, that His words are those of

Authoritative Certainty

He had come from Heaven, was familiar with all that went to make it, and was about to return thither. His purpose He could announce without either hesitancy or ambiguity. He is aware of the future. He knows because He has seen. He speaks because He knows. Men, on the contrary, make investigations, and they broadcast their deductions from the facts they have observed. They institute societies for psychical research, but their information is valueless. It is puerile, because it is not based on fact and experience. Christ was able to disclose the truth because of His own personal relationship to the matter He was announcing. His disclosures in a few sentences is worth all the volumes packed with the findings of human investigations. Its certainty should shame the crudities of their pronouncements.

Further, our Lord's assuring words are a tender evidence of

His Faithfulness and Trustworthiness.
He would not deceive His followers with a false hope. "If it were not so, I would have told you," are not the words of a mere enthusiast. Such is the veracity of His statement that not one need be deceived, but rather expect with ceratinty that all who love Him will follow Him into the Father's House, and find there the completest acceptance in Him their Lord. There, too, shall they find God perfectly accessible in the person of their Saviour, and find, besides, every hope of glory gained because His Word is true.

This announcement of Christ is no mere talk, but simple, unadorned truth, reliable because of His authority. So much so is this, that the Epistle to the Hebrews pictures the glorified Son before the Throne of God, in the midst of the great congregation—the many sons brought to Glory by the Captain of their Salvation, singing, "Behold I and the children whom Thou hast given Me" (Heb. 2. 13).

As assuring, too, are His further words, "I will come again and receive you unto Myself" (v. 3). How consoling are such words! "UNTO MYSELF," dispels every fear.

He is There to Welcome,
and the saint knows Him. But "unto Myself" is only a stage in the journey. The ultimate objective is the Father. He is the Heart of

the Home. Here Christ acts as Divine Usher. "I am the Way . . . no man cometh unto THE FATHER but by Me" (John 15. 6). What a welcome awaits the follower of the Son when he is brought unto the Father and presented "before the presence of His glory with exceeding joy" (Jude 24).

> "There no stranger God will meet thee,
> Stranger thou in courts above;
> He who to His rest will greet thee,
> Greets thee with a well-known love."

The heart of this revelation, then, is this:

Heaven is a place which Christ Went to Prepare.

What are we to understand by such a declaration? We must, as we have already insisted, discard notions of a material home, and therefore abandon the too prevalent idea that imagines that the words convey the thought of constant labour to bring an "imperfect structure" to a state of perfect habitation. We must think only of the moral perfections connected with the place. The preparation was that of His own Home-going as the Forerunner of the many who should follow. His entrance into the "Many Mansions" was to be the guarantee that entrance would not be denied to any who came to the Father by Him. There, too, He would await to introduce His own to their new surroundings and escort them through the abodes of the blessed in the companionship of the redeemed. *"With the*

*words of Christ there enters a conviction that
when we pass out of this life we shall find ourselves as much fuller of life and deeper in joy
as we are nearer God* . . . and that when we
come to the gates of God's dwelling it will
not be as the vagabond and beggar unknown
to the household, and who can give no good
account of himself, but as the child whose
room is ready for him, whose coming is expected
and prepared for, and who has indeed been
sent for."

To Christ, Heaven was

"My Father's House."

And He would make it that for His followers.
"Go," said He to Mary, "to My brethren, and
say unto them, I ascend unto My Father and
your Father" (John 20. 17). There, in such
a Home cannot be aught but satisfaction and
joy, bliss and perfect freedom. In that Heavenly Temple, built not with hands, will
dwell for ever the glory of God and His holiness.
And to such perfection will the spirits of just
men be brought that they will find every
aspiration attained and every spiritual im-
pulse satisfied. There, too, because it is the
Father's House, ample provision will be made
within the "many mansions" for all the children, and none will be afraid, but all will live
within the brightness of His countenance.
"There we shall be with cherubim and seraphim, creatures that will dazzle your eyes to
look upon them. There also you shall meet

with thousands and ten thousands that have gone before us to that place; none of them are hurtful, but loving and holy; every one walking in the sight of God, and standing in His presence with acceptance for ever.   In a word, there we shall see the elders with their golden crowns; there we shall see the holy virgins with their golden harps; there we shall see men that by the world were cut in pieces, burnt in flames, eaten of beasts, drowned in the seas, for the love they bore to the Lord of the place; all well and clothed with immortality as with a garment." *That Home which we call Heaven will be the most attractive spot in the Universe.*

Of the occupations and activities and

Joys of our Future State

the Master said nothing; but this surely we feel and know that all those proclivities and tendencies which link us with the earth now will for ever disappear, and the needs and necessities of a material life will pass as we enter, like Christ with a spiritual body into a realm of far-distances, emerging from the valley of the shadow into the glory that surrounds the House of the Lord.   We shall then be at Home with our Lord in the Father's House.

III. THE CITY OF THE LIVING GOD.

To impress the minds of His bewildered disciples with the sense of the freedom and society that they would enjoy in Heaven, the Lord used the simple synonym, "My Father's House." Notwithstanding the fact that their future abode would be a holy place like the Temple in the city, yet they were encouraged to think of it as a sphere of intimacies and fellowships because they would dwell together like a family brought to the Father through the love and labour of the Son.

As the company of the redeemed grew through the preaching of the Gospel, further revelations were given, and different similitudes were used to teach the saints truths concerning the life beyond time. Four symbols are thus found in the later writings of the New Testament, a Temple, a Bride, a Body, and a City.

The saints in Philippi, a Greek city which was recognised as a colony of Rome, looking to the Imperial City for all its laws and directions, were informed that

Their Citizenship was in Heaven

from whence they were to expect their Saviour. Hebrew Christians acquainted with the story of the Old Testament were reminded that they had "come to . . . the City of the living God, the Heavenly Jerusalem." When he wrote to the retrograde Galatians, the Apostle Paul, drawing a comparison between the economy of Law and the rule of Grace, introduced the idea of another city besides the earthly Jerusalem. It is called "the Jerusalem that is above," the counterpart in the Heavenly state of "the city that now is." Abraham, too, we are informed, "looked for

A City which hath Foundations,

whose Builder and Maker is God" (Heb. 11. 10). Strangers and pilgrims here, because they "have no continuing city," are exhorted to seek for "the City which is to come."

No reader of the Bible, therefore, need be astonished, as he peruses the pages of the Revelation and learns of things beyond death that the writer frequently draws his attention to the city which God has built. In chapter 21, it is seen as "the New Jerusalem which cometh down out of Heaven from God," while at the close of the Book the seer views from the "specular mount" a city of which he gives a ravishing description.

Our study of the subject may be greatly simplified if generalities are considered first. Thereafter it may be much easier to discover the interpretations of the details. These generalities consist of

Names and Comparisons.

This "city" state of existence is one of the items contained in the announcement, "Behold I make all things new" (Rev. 21. 5). In the Greek version of the New Testament two words are used for *new*. One of these refers to time, and conveys the idea of "*recent*." The other refers to quality, and bears the signification of "*fresh*." It is the latter word which is used throughout in the description of the New Jerusalem. The condition suggested, then, in the declaration is one of eternal freshness, stainless, incorruptibility, a state that corresponds with the announcement of Paul concerning the Church glorious that Christ will present it to Himself "without spot or wrinkle or any such thing" (Eph. 5. 27). John, too, informs us that into the city there will enter nothing that defileth.

The freshness of a new creation will characterise the Home of the Redeemed, and that freshness will never suffer decay or corruption. The rude tooth of time will play no havoc with its newness, nor will the stain of sin besmirch its undying glory and beauty. Eden and

More than Eden, will be Restored

without the remotest possibility of a malignant intruder spoiling the work which a Redeemer-God has wrought.

The city is called

"The New Jerusalem,

coming down from God out of Heaven." Jerusalem which now is (Gal. 4. 25) is a material city chosen of old as the earthly centre where Jehovah placed His Name, and in which the Temple was reared as the visible symbol of His presence. But this vision-city of the Revelation is not the evolution of man's progress. It is not of the earth, earthy; it descends from God out of Heaven. It is

Heavenly in its origin, its sphere, its characteristics, its inhabitants. It is the Home for those who, passing through the earth, thought of the end of life, and lived on earth in the light of eternity. That city-state is one of completest harmony with the will of God expressing itself in unabating worship of Him Whose glory is the light thereof.

A further appellation is

"The Holy City,"

"the Holy Jerusalem." Holiness is the ultimate goal of the Redeemer's activities, for in Him God chose saints "before the foundation of the world" that they might be "holy and without blame before Him" (Eph. 1. 4). Towards the achievement of that purpose the Holy Spirit is at present working in the obedient believer, so that each one doing the will of God and walking by the rule of the Spirit is "perfecting holiness in the fear of God."

On earth there can only be constant approximation to ideal perfection, but John here depicts a state in which the glorified saints dwell in "a holy city." Holiness is health, in the highest connotation of the term, when every faculty of body and mind is brought into unison with the will of God and works harmoniously in the circle of His beneficent purpose. To such complete accord with His will does God bring every one of His redeemed that the perfection for which they sighed and the holiness which they never attained will

8

become theirs, not through effort, but through the transforming power of His might.

"Prepared as a bride adorned for her husband," that city is further described as

"The Bride, the Lamb's Wife."

The imagery suggests not only the sacrificial bond that unites the saints to Christ, but also the idea of meticulous care in adornment for the day of espousals. The redeemed will reflect for ever not their own glories, but all the worth of their Redeemer, and will enjoy that unique fellowship suggested in the symbolism of "husband and wife." All the joy of a bride in her bridal attire for her nuptials will be theirs. All the hallowed intimacies of fellowship suggested by the conjugal tie will be theirs. Unchanging affection and unstinted loyalty will mark the Heavenly state.

"The Tabernacle of God"

is a further descriptive metaphor. Paul employs the imagery of a temple when he writes to the Ephesians whose city housed the famous image of Diana in the magnificent temple dedicated to her worship. They thought of a deity presiding within the vast edifice, and Paul, quick to make use of the mental content of his readers in conveying spiritual truths, declared that God was building an invisible structure, rearing a spiritual edifice upon Christ, the Chief Corner Stone, "in whom the whole building, fitly framed together groweth unto an holy temple in the Lord, in whom ye also are builded together for an habitation of God through the Spirit" (Eph. 2. 21, 22).

But John saw in his vision, not a temple, but a tabernacle. Such a metaphor can convey to Bible students only one message. The Shekinah glory of Jehovah dwelt upon the wilderness structure of old, and became the symbol of the presence of God. By that glory-cloud the Presence seemed to be localised, and the Israelites were made aware of Jehovah's nearness. But over Israel's later history had to be written Ichabod. God, however, visited His people again, and it is the writer of the Apocalypse who defines that visitation in these terms: "And the Word became flesh and tabernacled among us, and we beheld His glory" (John 1. 14). Now he sees the "tabernacle of God" descending out of Heaven and having the glory of God; the saints become the habitation of God, for He tabernacles with them. Subsequently John tells us that he saw "no temple therein; for the Lord God Almighty and the Lamb are the Temple" (Rev. 21. 22). God is everywhere accessible to every one, but that right of access has been procured only through sacrifice. The Divine presence is diffused equally, and there is no need for aids in that perfect state, when God through the Lamb makes Himself known without intermediary to all the saints.

Heaven, then, will be a state in which

The Saints will Reach Spiritual Perfection, will retain throughout eternity the marks of unfading freshness, will have unimpeded access to God through the Lamb, will reflect the moral glories of their Redeemer, and, dwelling together as an habitation of God through the Spirit, will perform His will with perfect devotion and unstained holiness.

IV. DETAILS OF THE HEAVENLY CITY.

Having discussed briefly the general characteristics of the city, it may be of interest to seek to learn somewhat of the more particular details with which the vision furnishes us. In doing so our present purpose may be the better served if the details are taken, not so much in the order in which they are given, but grouped together so as to impress upon our minds certain outstanding features of that future state.

It will have been observed by careful readers that the description deals more at length with the *external* aspect of the City than with those which are internal. The inhabitants are not described, perhaps, because they are already referred to in the description of the City itself. Think, however, of those who are within this City.

The Throne of God and of the Lamb

are there. In chapter 4 the vision is of the Throne of God in all its unsullied governmental splendour, a splendour of holiness which repels everything that is not in the strictest harmony therewith.   In chapter 5 the Lamb approaches that Throne, associates Himself therewith and now the ideas are combined, and within the eternal City there is seen the "Throne of God and of the Lamb," one throne, one centre of government with a dual character.

The story of the Bible centres round the Throne of God.   It is the story of the warring of God against sin and rebellion as He establishes His Throne upon justice and mercy, ruling and yet saving a people out of disaster. Rebellion against God and His Throne has characterised man since the Devil and his angels, themselves fallen from Heaven by an act of impious revolt, seduced him from his loyalty and led him into disobedience.

The Book of the Revelation details

The Final Catastrophe

which overtakes these wicked spirits and unrepentant men, and discloses the fact that the Throne of God remains immovably fixed in Heaven, retains its impregnable character in spite of malicious assault and persistent disobedience, and in the end centralises the government of the New Heavens and the New Earth.   But these governmental dealings are eternally associated with "the Lamb." Glory and grace, power and sacrifice, are harmoniously combined and in perfect unison.

Attention is focused upon the fact that

Heaven is Redolent with Sacrifice,

as prominence is given to the Lamb.   The city is called "the Lamb's wife," the apostles are "the apostles of the Lamb," "the Lord God Almighty and the Lamb are the temple" of the City, only those which "are written in the Lamb's book of life," are allowed access to the City, while the Lamb is the lamp of the Glory, which lightens the City.

Thus the government of God, established through grace and on the ground of sacrifice, is acknowledged throughout the vast domain as all rejoice around the Throne and declare "the Lamb is all the glory of Immanuel's Land."

This idea of the perfection of the Divine government is further suggested by the employment of

The Numerical Symbol, Twelve.

Here we read of twelve gates, twelve angels, twelve apostles, twelve thousand furlongs, one hundred and forty and four cubits, twelve foundation stones, twelve pearls and twelve manner of fruits.   The harmonious outworking of God's eternal purpose has reached its full fruition, every evil has been banished, righteous government has been established beyond assault and the glory of it all is centred in the Lamb.

Associated with the Throne, as being intimately connected with the governmental dealings of God, are

The Tree of Life

and the River of Water of Life. Such expression cannot fail to drive us back to the story of man's first home—Eden.

Sin, in its foul disobedient act, shattered the primitive bliss, because it was disloyalty to the Throne, an affront to the government of God. Now the consequences of the Fall have been removed, Eden, and more than Eden, has been restored, and man, redeemed from the curse, has entered into a state of which his first home was but a picture.

Life in all its fulness (fruit and water), with endless opportunity to express its vitality, without possibility of decay and weariness, maintained in incorruptible purity and perennial freshness, with the bloom of a new creation for ever in its constitution, is the portion of every one. Proceeding as it does from the Throne of God and of the Lamb, the River of Life carries with it from God exhaustless tides of supply for all the redeemed, so that their "health" is guaranteed for ever, for the fruits of the tree speaks of kindly variety in the fulness of Divine knowledge. Here there is no tree of the knowledge of good and evil, for evil has been excluded for ever, and all knowledge is wrapt up in the endless unfolding of the Divine wisdom of which the Lamb is the embodiment. And because that is so there shall be no more curse. The unadorned statement conveys its own volume of truth, which needs no expansion.

"No more curse."
Angels, patriarchs, and

Apostles are There.

What a company! The angels are those who
kept their first estate and fell not. They have
unceasingly lived within the presence of
Jehovah, waiting to do His will, posting "o'er
land and ocean without rest." They have
required no physical transformation to fit them
for this eternal abode. "At the gates" of the
City they stand in readiness to carry out each
behest of their Lord, a picture of unceasing
service ungrudgingly performed. Angelic mini-
strations will not cease throughout the eternal
state.

Here, too, are those who, like Abraham,

The Father of the Faithful,

desired "a better country, that is a Heavenly:
wherefore God is not ashamed to be called their
God, for He hath prepared for them a City"
(Heb. 11. 16), those who, like Simeon and
Anna, longed for the salvation of God, or looked
for redemption in Israel. What a galaxy of
saints redeemed out of Israel in virtue of the
Blood of Christ.

Prominence, however, is reserved for the

"Foundations of the City,"

for on these are inscribed the names of the
twelve apostles of the Lamb. Is not that a
symbolic manner of intimating a fact already

plainly stated by the Apostle Paul? "Ye are fellow-citizens with the saints, . . . and are built upon the foundation of the apostles and prophets, Jesus Christ Himself being the chief corner stone" (Eph. 2. 19, 20).

Out of every kindred, tribe, people, and nation, have been gathered together the hosts of the redeemed, displaying in all their beauty and variety the glories of God, their Redeemer, Who has made them "all one in Christ Jesus," and has granted them a place in that City in which each one, retaining his own individuality, yet resplendent with glory, will be to the praise of His grace. In no other way, perhaps, could the Divine Spirit have conveyed to our minds such a transporting picture of the everlasting splendour of the saints in their corporate life, as by this display of magnificence in the precious stones that reflect the glory of God.

Two outstanding phrases are used to describe the appearance of the city.

"The City Lieth Foursquare,"

and "the city was like unto pure gold, clear as crystal." Much speculation has surrounded the interpretation of the former statement along with the description given supplementary to it. Literalists have calculated the dimensions of the city, and, assigning so many square feet per inhabitant, have arrived at the population of 39,204,000,000 people. Surely that is not the intention of the Holy Spirit! Since the length, breadth, and height of it are equal, there is presented the symbol of perfect symmetry, in which all is in true proportion, and viewed from any side displays the completeness of the Divine ideal without distortion of any kind.

Again, there is a divergence of opinion as to whether the shape is cubical or pyramidal. No hint is given as to which is correct, for it could be either without violation of the dimensions given. The writer's opinion, notwithstanding the beauty attached to some interpretations demanding the pyramidal form, is that the shape is that of a cube. So frequently does the seer draw attention to the fact that the City has the glory of God upon it, that it seems justifiable to conclude that he had in his vision something which reminded him of the innermost sanctuary of the Temple which was a cube. That was the symbol of the dwelling place of Jehovah, and was associated in a Jewish mind with the manifestation of His glory. Here the whole City is cubical in form, suggesting what other statements infer that the City itself is the Temple of Jehovah, or to use words already familiar, "the tabernacle of God is with men." God is in the midst, dwelling with His people, their God.

Twice Gold is Mentioned

in the description of the City, once as to its general appearance, and a second time when we read: "And the street of the City was pure gold, as it were transparent glass." Purity is stamped on the vision from beginning to end.

The whole aspect of the City betokens a display of Divine righteousness reflected in every transaction of the inhabitants. Transparency characterises all. Men to-day hide themselves from their neighbours; in that day there will be no need for darkness, for the glory of God lightens every corner of the City, and the transparency of the gold of the street suggests that in all work, walk, and ways there will be unsullied righteousness and untarnished holiness. *What a state*!

V. **THE CONSUMMATION**.

It is but fitting that certain details should be reserved for the last, reminding us of what are not to be found within that "city-state."

A String of Negatives

throws into vivid relief the perfect bliss of the home to which Christ will take His own. "There shall be no more death, neither sorrow, nor crying, neither shall there be any more pain." These gone, and gone for ever, we can understand how God shall wipe away all tears from every eye. He does so by removing the causes of sorrow, so that tears there are none. Two quotations may fitly bring this chapter to a close. The first is taken from Dr. Pierson's "God's Living Oracles":

"The Grand Sevenfold Consummation

of all the Redemption plan is given in the twenty-second chapter of Revelation:

"'And there shall be no more curse'—*Perfect sinlessness.*

"'And the throne of God and of the Lamb shall be in it'—*Perfect authority.*

"'And His servants shall serve Him'—*Perfect obedience.*

"'And they shall see His face'—*Perfect communion.*

"'And His Name shall be in their foreheads'—*Perfect consecration.*

"'And there shall be no night there'—*Perfect blessedness.*

"'And they shall reign for ever and ever'—*Perfect glory.*

"What visions of such sevenfold perfection are found anywhere outside of the Oracles of God!"

"The light of Heaven," writes someone, "is the face of Jesus, the joy of Heaven is the presence of Jesus, the melody of Heaven the Name of Jesus, the harmony of Heaven the praise of Jesus, the theme of Heaven the work of Jesus, the employment of Heaven the service of Jesus, the fulness of Heaven, JESUS HIMSELF."

To that bliss there will be no end, for not only are all defilements excluded, but the Spirit declares that "there shall in no wise enter into it any thing that defileth, neither whatsoever worketh abomination, or maketh a lie" (Rev. 21. 27).

History began in a garden, it ends in a garden city. The first city was built by the first murderer to hide himself therein, the last city is one into which no stain of any kind will find entrance. This garden city is the Home of God and the redeemed, a place of dazzling splendour, of unassailable security, of marvellous accessibility, of impregnable strength, of inconceivable compass, of ravishing beauty, of unparalleled blessedness, of stainless purity, with guarded entrance, and withal, redolent with the memory of the death of the Lamb.

CHAPTER XII

A Concise Study of Heaven

By S. LAVERY, Lisburn

WE are entirely dependent upon the Word of God for all our knowledge of Heaven and from it we learn Who created it, where it is, who will be there, who will not be there, the bliss of it, and the way to it. In our consideration of this all-important subject, for the sake of simplicity we will look at it under the following headings:

1. **The Person Who Created It**. See Gen. 1. 1; Psa. 8. 3; Isa. 40. 22; Rev. 10. 6.

2. **The Position of It**. Heaven is a place, not merely a state or condition. The position of it is "up" or "above." See *e.g.*, Josh. 8. 20; Jud. 20. 40; 2 Kings 2. 1; Psa. 103. 11; 139. 8; Prov. 30. 4; Amos 9. 2; Mark 6. 41; 16. 19; Luke 9. 6; 24. 51; Acts 1. 9, 10, 11, 22; 2. 19; 7. 55; 10. 16; 11. 10; Eph. 4. 8-10; Rev. 11. 12.

3. **The People Who will be in It**.

God the Father (Psa. 115. 3; Matt. 6. 9). The One Who provided the sacrifice in the Person of Christ.

God the Son (John 3. 13; 1 Thess. 4. 16, 17). The One Who came in wondrous grace and voluntarily died on the Cross, Who is now the Intercessor and Advocate of His people in Heaven.

God the Holy Ghost.   The One Who convicted, regenerated, indwelt the saints of this present age, and Who also was their Guide and Leader.

The Angels.   Matt. 18. 10; 24. 36.

The Old Testament Saints saved in view of the sacrifice of Christ.

Those saved during the Lord's earthly ministry. These will include apostles, prophets, publicans, and sinners of every class.

The saints of the present age, who were saved through the accomplished work on Calvary. These will include evangelists, pastors, teachers and all the saints who have trusted in the Lord Jesus Christ.

Those martyred during the dark days of the tribulation period.   Rev. 20. 4.

4. **The People who will not be in Heaven**. See 1 Cor. 6. 9; Gal. 5. 21; Eph. 5. 5; Rev. 21. 8; 22. 15.

5. **The Perfect Bliss of Heaven**.   See *e.g.*, Psa. 16. 11; Rev. 7. 16; 21. 4.   What a wonderful place it is, without tears, sorrow, disease, or pain, and where partings will be no more.

6. **The Person Who is the Way to Heaven**. The Lord Jesus Christ is the Way to Heaven, the Father's House.   He said, "I am the Way . . . no man cometh unto the Father but by Me" (John 14. 6).   He by His sacrifice on Calvary's cruel Cross has made it possible for a righteous God to admit through Heaven's portals sinners saved by grace.   Will you be there?   If not, why not?

No Nails!

OR, THINGS NOT IN HEAVEN.

I SHALL not see sad countenances there,
    The latest tear I meet on earth will be
The last I know; unless the vision fair
    Of my beloved Lord arouses me
To tears of love and unrestrained delight.
    No grief shall grip the heart, or numb the mind,
No darkness, nor the terrors of the night
    Shall there be known: I leave such things behind.
Partings shall be no more, and lonely hours,
    For I shall serve the Lord, and see His face,
And wander in a wilderness of flowers
    With saints and angels, called from every race.
Nor do I hope to find amongst that band,
    Those full of pride, dictators, Sadducees,
Blind leaders of the blind; at God's right hand
    No place is found, no Crown, for such as these.
Not all who said, "Lord! Lord!" their head shall lay
    Upon His breast; and not a soul is found
That has attained thereto some other way
    Than by His Blood, the one redemption-ground.
Sin and deceit are flown far, far away,
    Things of the past, and death, and strife, and war
Shall not disturb the happiness, for they
    Have given place to peace for evermore.
No Cross shall rear its shape, forbidding, grim,
    Upon a hill in Heaven, for all are free.
And there will be no nails, no nails for Him,
    The altogether lovely.   I shall see
Only the scars they left on each dear limb,
    A testimonial for eternity!   V. TOPPS.